German

Rachel Aukett

Published by BBC Worldwide Ltd,
Woodlands, 80 Wood Lane, London W12 0TT

First published 2002; reprinted 2003, June 2004, 2005

© Rachel Aukett/BBC Worldwide Ltd, 2002
All rights reserved.

ISBN: 0 563 50127 8

Colour reproduction by Tien Wah Press Pte Ltd, Singapore
Printed and bound by Tien Wah Press Pte Ltd, Singapore

Contents

Introduction

Using this book to revise

About Bitesize

GCSE Bitesize is a revision service designed to help you achieve success at GCSE. There are books, television programmes and a website, each of which provides a separate resource designed to help you get the best results.

TV programmes are available on video through your school or you can find out transmission times by calling 08700 100 222.

The website can be found at http://www.bbc.co.uk/schools/gcsebitesize/

About this book

This book is your all-in-one revision companion for GCSE.
It gives you the three things you need for successful revision:

1 **Every topic clearly organised and explained in four main chapters:** My world, Holiday time and travel, Work and lifestyle and Young person in society.

2 **The key vocabulary and grammar pulled out for quick and easy revision reference:** both in the four main chapters and in the extra sections at the end of the book.

3 **All the practice you need:** in the 'check' questions in the margins, in the practice questions at the end of each topic area, and in the exam practice section at the end of this book.

Each chapter is organised in the same way:

■ **Key vocabulary and phrases** broken down into smaller topic areas, with suggestions for learning the vocabulary and activities to practise it.

■ **The Bare Bones** – a summary of the main points – a good way to check what you know.

■ **Key ideas** highlighted throughout.

■ **Check questions** in the margin – have you understood this bit?

About this book *continued*

- **Grammar boxes** highlighting the key grammar you need to know.

- **Remember tips** in the margin - extra advice on this section of the topic.

- **Practice questions** at the end of each topic to check your understanding.

The extra sections at the back of this book will help you to check your progress and be confident that you know your stuff:

- **Listening** - a chapter of listening activities which you can do if you have a copy of the Bitesize German video (see facing page for details of how to get it).

- **Exam questions and model answers** – example exam questions for Listening, Speaking, Reading and Writing – with model answers to help you get full marks.

- **Topic checker** - quick-fire questions on all your topics. See how many you can answer after you've revised a chapter.

- **Complete the grammar** - another resource for you to use as you revise: fill in the gaps to complete the key grammar.

- **Last-minute learner** - a mini-book that you can cut out containing all the most important vocabulary and phrases in just four pages.

- **Answers** - check all your answers to the activities in the book.

Planning your revision

When are your GCSE German exams? (Remember, there are four exams: Listening, Speaking, Reading AND Writing.) Next month? Next year?

The first thing you need to do is work out how many days there are to go. If there's eighty days, that means you could spend twenty days on each of the four sections. You've got other subjects to think about as well, of course, so spread the revision out in the best way for you. Writing down an action plan for yourself will help you focus on what you need to do between now and the exam itself.

Once you've drawn up your revision timetable, you can start your actual work. When you revise, make sure that:

- you've got a quiet place to work

- you've got everything you need in the room – books, pens, paper, the video, a dictionary . . .

- you don't get distracted by computer games, the TV, radio, magazines . . .

- you don't revise for too long without a break – set a time-limit for yourself to make sure that you keep fresh and motivated.

On the day

Make sure that you know the exact day, time and place for each of your German exams. Get to the exam room in good time and make sure that you've got a pen and a pencil with you. You might also like to take a ruler, a rubber, a dictionary (if your school isn't providing them) and a good-luck mascot.

On your way to the exam, go through a few key points in German – for instance, you could count to 50, say a bit about yourself or listen to a German cassette. There's not much point trying to learn new things in the few hours before the exam – so just concentrate on revising a bit to get yourself into a 'German' mood.

The German exam

Nobody expects you to know everything on the day of your exam, but see if you can manage to do the following:

■ say two or three sentences about yourself in German

■ know your numbers to fifty (and above if possible)

■ know some important key phrases.

Good luck with your revision – and good luck in your exam!

THE BARE

BONES

➤ Conversations, forms and letters about yourself and your family often appear in the exam.
➤ Make sure you know the alphabet, the months, the seasons and numbers 1–100.

A About you

SPEAK

1 <u>Lies das Gespräch unten.</u>
Read the conversation below.

✪ *Wie heißt du mit Vornamen?*
✷ Ich heiße Maria.
✪ *Dein Familienname?*
✷ Schmidt.
✪ *Kannst du das buchstabieren?*
✷ S-C-H-M-I-D-T.

✪ *Wie alt bist du?*
✷ Fünfzehn Jahre alt.
✪ *Wann hast du Geburtstag?*
✷ Ich habe am fünfzehnten Januar Geburtstag.

Q Reply to each question with your own personal information. Practise the dialogue with a friend.

Q Spell your name in German (see page 12).

2 <u>Lies die Mitgliedsliste des Jugendklubs und beantworte die Fragen für jede Person.</u>
Read the youth club register and answer the questions above for each person.

FAMILIENNAME	VORNAME	ALTER	GEBURTSDATUM
1 Schmidt	Katharina	15	15.1
2 Scherer	Elisabeth	13	9.10
3 Weingartner	Axel	12	17.7
4 Marienberg	Tobias	17	31.3

B Describing yourself

WRITE

1 <u>Wie siehst du aus? Schreibe es auf!</u>
What do you look like? Write it down!

Ich bin	groß/klein/mittelgroß/dick/schlank.
Meine Haare sind	dunkelbraun/hellbraun/schwarz/ blond/rot. kurz/lang. glatt/lockig.
Meine Augen sind	braun/grün/blau.

B **2** <u>Beschreibe diese Leute.</u>
Describe these people.

Q Practise describing the appearance of every member of your family.

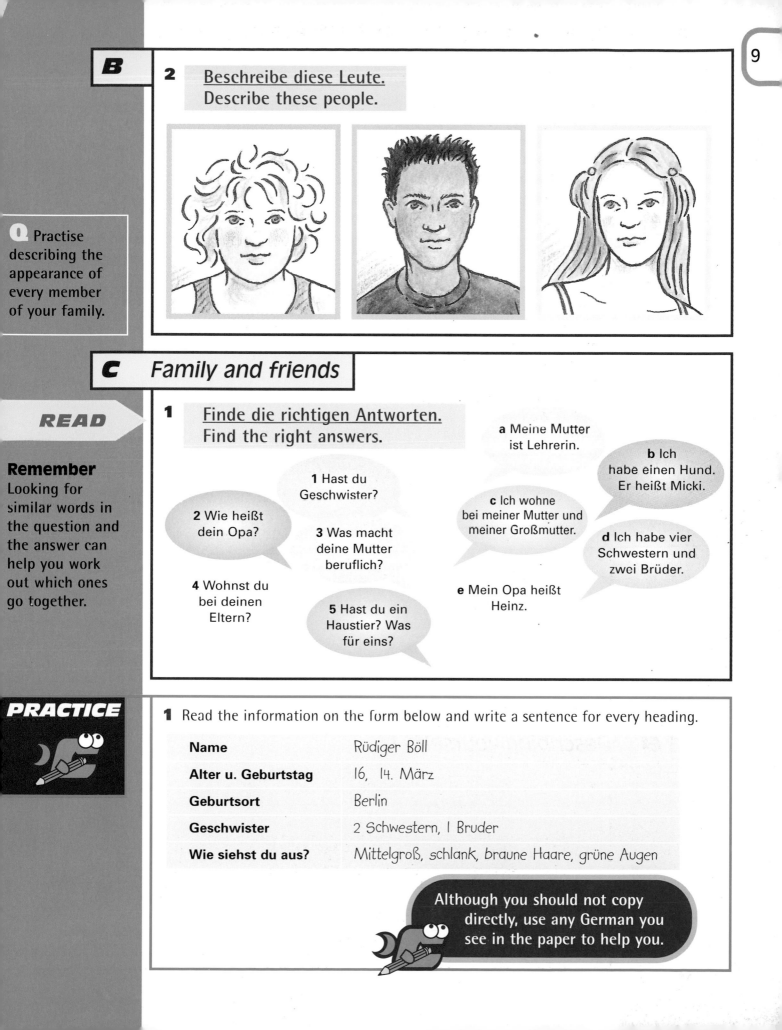

C Family and friends

READ

Remember
Looking for similar words in the question and the answer can help you work out which ones go together.

1 <u>Finde die richtigen Antworten.</u>
Find the right answers.

1 Hast du Geschwister?

2 Wie heißt dein Opa?

3 Was macht deine Mutter beruflich?

4 Wohnst du bei deinen Eltern?

5 Hast du ein Haustier? Was für eins?

a Meine Mutter ist Lehrerin.

b Ich habe einen Hund. Er heißt Micki.

c Ich wohne bei meiner Mutter und meiner Großmutter.

d Ich habe vier Schwestern und zwei Brüder.

e Mein Opa heißt Heinz.

PRACTICE

1 Read the information on the form below and write a sentence for every heading.

Name	Rüdiger Böll
Alter u. Geburtstag	16, 14. März
Geburtsort	Berlin
Geschwister	2 Schwestern, 1 Bruder
Wie siehst du aus?	Mittelgroß, schlank, braune Haare, grüne Augen

Although you should not copy directly, use any German you see in the paper to help you.

Going out

THE BARE BONES

➤ For the exam, you should know how to talk or write about going out, and how to ask someone to go out with you.

➤ To get a C grade or above, it is important that you can speak using three tenses: past, present and future. In this section, you will see the simple future.

A Who do you go out with?

SPEAK

1 <u>Lies das Diagramm. Mit wem gehst du gern aus? Warum?</u>
Read the grid. Who do you like to go out with and why?

Remember
When you use mit it changes the word for 'the' (see Grammar page 49).

Q Describe your favourite person and say why you like spending time with him/her.

| Ich verbringe gern Zeit mit | meiner Mutter/Kusine/ Schwester/Freundin/ Oma/Tante | weil sie | toll komisch interessant lustig nett | ist. |
| | meinem Vater/Cousin/ Bruder/Freund/ Opa/Onkel | weil er | freundlich pünktlich reich humorvoll | |

Beispiel: Ich verbringe gern Zeit mit meiner Tante, weil sie reich ist!

B Where would you go?

WRITE

1 <u>Wo machen sie das? Fülle die Lücken aus.</u>
Where do they do that? Fill the gaps.

auf dem Land   ins Freibad

ins Hallenbad   ins Kino

Q What do you like to do? Who do you like doing it with? Where do you do it?

a Meine Mutter liebt frische Luft. Am Wochenende will sie _____ mit der Familie und unserem Hund spazieren gehen.

b Mein Onkel Stefan liebt das Wasser. Wir fahren oft mit ihm _____. Er schwimmt sehr gern und ist am liebsten draußen.

c Meine Freunde und ich gehen oft in die Stadt. Wir lieben James Bond und alle Actionfilme. Samstagnachmittags gehen wir manchmal _____.

C Arranging to go out

WRITE

WRITE

1 Schreibe diese Einladungen richtig auf.
Write these invitations out in full.

Remember
The simple future tense is made of words which indicate you are talking about the future + the present tense.

An:	Sonja	Max	Alexia
Wann?	Sa.	Mo.	Di.
Was?	Disko	Theater	Spazieren
Treffpunkt	vor dem Bahnhof	auf der Brücke	neben dem Supermarkt
Uhrzeit	19:00	19:30	11:00
Absender	Michael, Micki, Sandra	Simone	Kurt

Beispiel:

Liebe Sonja!

Am Samstagabend gehen wir in die Disko. Hast du Lust mitzukommen?
Wir treffen uns um 19:00 Uhr vor dem Bahnhof. Komm mit!

Tschüs!

Micki, Michael und Sandra

Q Practise arranging to go out with someone – agree the time, place and what you are going to do – on the phone!

PRACTICE

1 Call your German pen pal and invite her to go to the cinema with you.

- Say hello and who you want to speak to.
- Ask if she would like to come with you to the cinema.
- Tell her where to meet you.
- Tell her when to meet you.
- Say goodbye.

In the exam, be careful that you don't miss out any of the things you have been asked to do!

Vocabulary

A Self, family and friends

Wie heißt du?	What's your name?
Ich heiße .../Mein Name ist ...	I'm called .../My name is ...
Wie alt bist du?	How old are you?
Ich bin ... Jahre alt.	I'm ... years old.
Ich habe am ... Geburtstag.	My birthday is on ...
Ich trage eine Brille.	I wear glasses.
Hast du Geschwister?	Have you got any brothers and sisters?
Ich bin Einzelkind.	I'm an only child.
Ich habe eine Schwester/einen Bruder.	I've got a sister/a brother.
Hast du Haustiere?	Have you got any pets?
Ich habe einen Hund/eine Katze/eine Maus ...	I've got a dog/cat/mouse ...

a (ah)	g (gay)	m (as English)	s (as English)	y (oopsilon)
b (bay)	h (ha)	n (as English)	t (tay)	z (tsett)
c (tsay)	i (ee)	o (or)	u (oo)	ß (s-tsett)
d (day)	j (yot)	p (pay)	v (fow)	ä (eh)
e (ay)	k (ka)	q (koo)	w (vay)	ö (er)
f (as English)	l (as English)	r (air)	x (eeks)	ü (eu)

Remember
To help you remember gender (der, die, das) put words which are the same together (e.g. all der words together, etc.).

der Bruder	brother	das Mädchen	girl
der Cousin	boy cousin	die Mutter	mother
die Eltern	parents	der Onkel	uncle
die Großeltern	grandparents	die Schwester	sister
die Großmutter	grandmother	der Sohn	son
der Großvater	grandfather	der Stiefbruder	step-brother
der Halbbruder	half-brother	die Stiefschwester	step-sister
die Halbschwester	half-sister	die Tante	aunt
das Kind	child	die Tochter	daughter
die Kusine	girl cousin	der Zwilling	twin

Q Draw your own family tree. Can you introduce all the members of your family in German?

Q Describe your favourite person's character.

Was machst du in deiner Freizeit/am Wochenende?	What do you do in your free time/ at the weekend?
Ich treffe mich mit Freunden.	I meet my friends.
Ich tanze sehr gern.	I like dancing very much.
Ich fahre lieber Rad.	I prefer cycling
Das meine ich auch.	I agree.
Ich spiele nicht gern Tischtennis.	I don't like playing table tennis.
Ich auch nicht.	Neither do I.
Freitags gehe ich in die Disko.	I go to the disco on Fridays.
Letzten Samstag habe ich Fußball gespielt.	I played football last Saturday.
Ich gehe in die Stadt.	I go into town.
Was kann man hier machen?	What's there to do here?
Man kann/Du kannst spazierengehen/ ins Kino gehen ...	You can go for a walk/ to the cinema ...
Wo/Wann treffen wir uns?	Where/when shall we meet?
Das freut mich.	That pleases me./I'm glad.

B Going out

in die Disko	*to the disco (going there)*	toll	*great*
in der Disko	*at the disco (already there)*	interessant	*interesting*
		lustig	*funny*
auf dem Land	*in the country*	nett	*nice*
auf dem Strand	*on the beach*	freundlich	*friendly*
ins Hallenbad/	*to the indoor pool/*	pünktlich	*on time/punctual*
ins Freibad	*open-air pool*	reich	*rich*
		humorvoll	*humorous*

Grammar

C Nouns

1 Nouns (people, places or things) in German always begin with a capital letter.

Hier ist mein Bruder.   Die Katze heißt Micki.

2 Nouns in German are either masculine, feminine or neuter. The word for **a** or **the** changes as follows:

Masculine	**Ein** Mann sitzt im Bus.	A man is sitting on the bus.
	Der Mann heißt Ulrich.	The man is called Ulrich.
Feminine	**Eine** Frau sitzt im Bus.	A woman is sitting on the bus.
	Die Frau heißt Ulla.	The woman is called Ulla.
Neuter	**Ein** Haus liegt in der Stadt.	A house is in the city.
	Das Haus liegt in der Stadt.	The house is in the city.

3 If a word is made of two smaller words, the last word tells you the gender:

Die Hand + der Schuh = der Handschuh

Remember
There are more masculine nouns than either feminine or neuter ones, and the only way to know which is which is to learn them.

D Du or Sie?

1 Do you remember when to use **du** and **Sie**? Let's recap:

du → a child, a friend, family member

Sie → an adult or adults

Q Would you use **du** or **Sie** to address: your German teacher; your aunt; Frau May's baby?

 # Interests and hobbies

THE BARE BONES

➤ It is important that you know how to speak and write about hobbies and leisure activities for the exam.

➤ Make sure that you know the days of the week and can use the correct word order when these (or any other time words) come first in a sentence.

A Hobbies

WRITE

Remember
All nouns in German have a capital letter at the beginning.

Q How many other hobbies and pastimes can you name?

1 <u>Schreibe diese Hobbys richtig auf.</u>
Unjumble these hobbies.

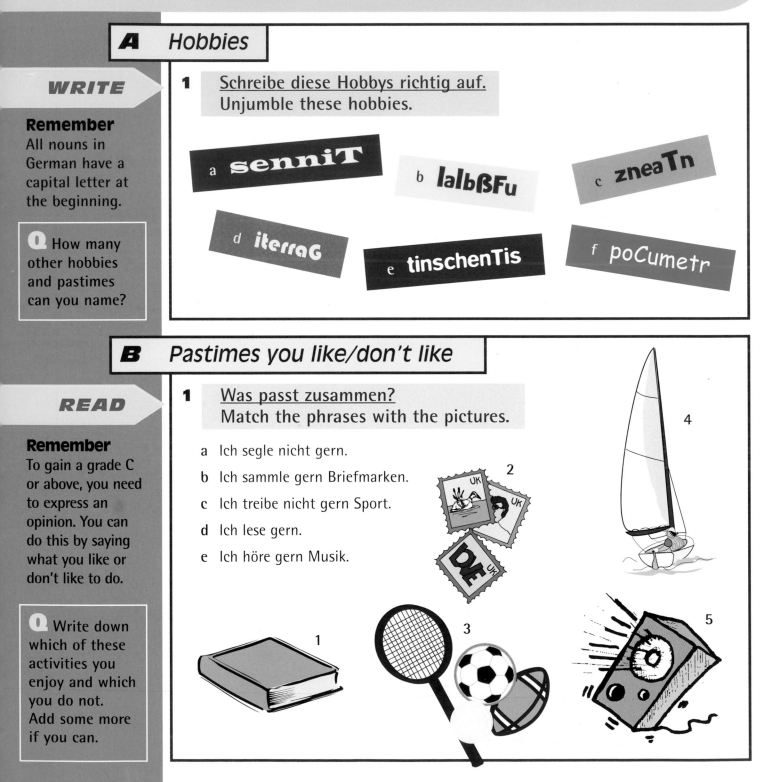

a **senniT**

b **lalbßFu**

c **zneaTn**

d **iterraG**

e **tinschenTis**

f **poCumetr**

B Pastimes you like/don't like

READ

Remember
To gain a grade C or above, you need to express an opinion. You can do this by saying what you like or don't like to do.

Q Write down which of these activities you enjoy and which you do not. Add some more if you can.

1 <u>Was passt zusammen?</u>
Match the phrases with the pictures.

a Ich segle nicht gern.

b Ich sammle gern Briefmarken.

c Ich treibe nicht gern Sport.

d Ich lese gern.

e Ich höre gern Musik.

C When you do your hobby

1 <u>Was machst du abends?</u>
What do you do in the evening? Use the information given.

Montag	Dienstag	Mittwoch	Donnerstag	Freitag
Musik hören	lesen	schwimmen	Tennis	schlafen!

Beispiel: Am **Montag** höre ich Musik. **Montags** mache ich das immer.

D Putting it all together

1 <u>Lies den Text und kreuze (X) an, was richtig (R), falsch (F) oder nicht im Text (N) ist.</u>
Read the text and then say whether the statement is true (R), false (F) or not in the text (N).

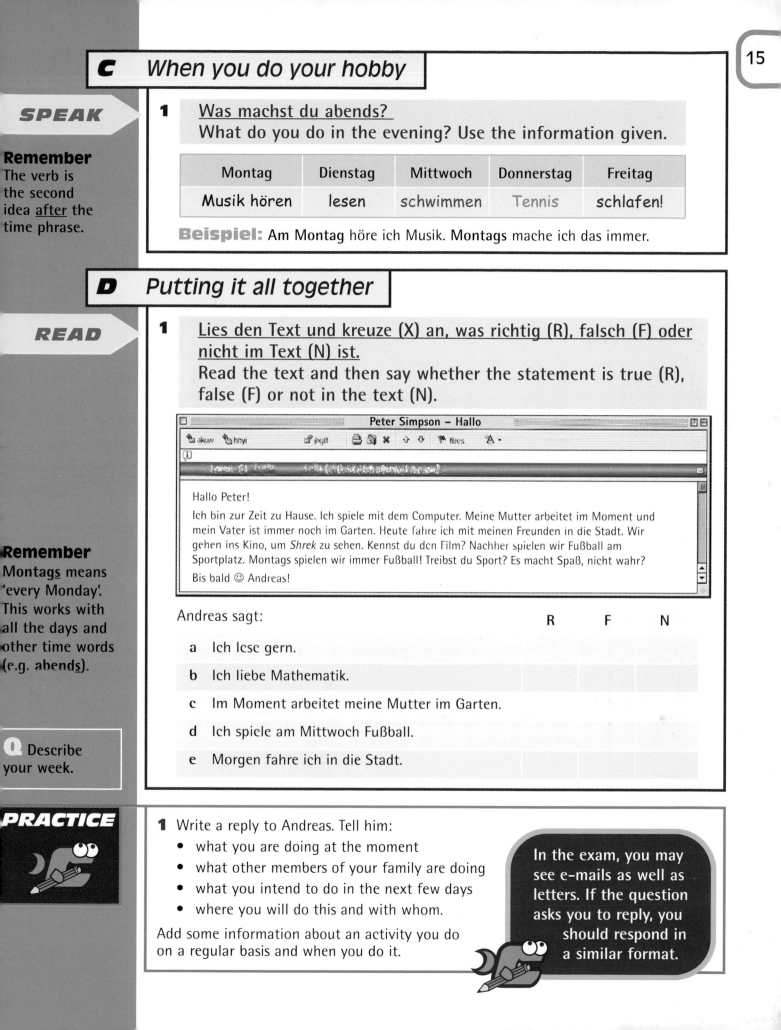

> Peter Simpson – Hallo
>
> Hallo Peter!
> Ich bin zur Zeit zu Hause. Ich spiele mit dem Computer. Meine Mutter arbeitet im Moment und mein Vater ist immer noch im Garten. Heute fahre ich mit meinen Freunden in die Stadt. Wir gehen ins Kino, um *Shrek* zu sehen. Kennst du den Film? Nachher spielen wir Fußball am Sportplatz. Montags spielen wir immer Fußball! Treibst du Sport? Es macht Spaß, nicht wahr?
> Bis bald ☺ Andreas!

Andreas sagt: R   F   N

a   Ich lese gern.

b   Ich liebe Mathematik.

c   Im Moment arbeitet meine Mutter im Garten.

d   Ich spiele am Mittwoch Fußball.

e   Morgen fahre ich in die Stadt.

1 Write a reply to Andreas. Tell him:
- what you are doing at the moment
- what other members of your family are doing
- what you intend to do in the next few days
- where you will do this and with whom.

Add some information about an activity you do on a regular basis and when you do it.

> In the exam, you may see e-mails as well as letters. If the question asks you to reply, you should respond in a similar format.

THE BARE BONES

➤ In the exam, you may be asked to describe your house and garden, and what is in your room.

➤ You might have to compare living in the country and in a city or town.

➤ You should also be able to describe your town and local area.

A Your room

SPEAK

1 <u>Schreibe diese Wörter richtig auf. Verbinde sie mit dem richtigen Bild.</u>
Unjumble the words and match them to the pictures.

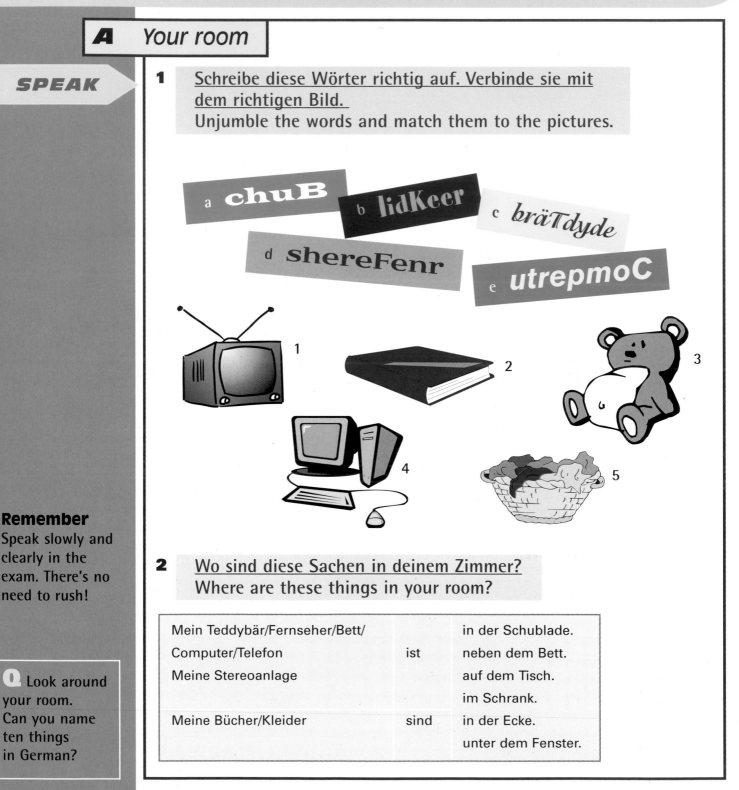

a chuB

b lidKeer

c bräTdyde

d shereFenr

e utrepmoC

Remember
Speak slowly and clearly in the exam. There's no need to rush!

Q Look around your room. Can you name ten things in German?

2 <u>Wo sind diese Sachen in deinem Zimmer?</u>
Where are these things in your room?

Mein Teddybär/Fernseher/Bett/		in der Schublade.
Computer/Telefon	ist	neben dem Bett.
Meine Stereoanlage		auf dem Tisch.
		im Schrank.
Meine Bücher/Kleider	sind	in der Ecke.
		unter dem Fenster.

B Your local area

WRITE

1 <u>Beschreibe ich das Leben auf dem Land oder in der Stadt?</u>
Am I describing life in the country or the town?

a. Da gibt es sehr viel zu tun.

b. Wir können immer ins Kino, ins Theater oder in die Disko gehen. Es ist nicht weit.

c. Man muss immer mit dem Auto fahren, um etwas Interessantes zu unternehmen.

d. Die Luft ist frisch und gesund.

Q Would you prefer to live in the country or the town? Why?

2 <u>Welche Sätze sind Vorteile? Welche sind Nachteile?</u>
Decide if each phrase is an advantage or a disadvantage.

C Your house

READ

1 <u>Fülle die Lücken aus.</u>
Read Peter's description of his house and fill in the gaps.

Remember
You don't have to understand every word in a text. Diagrams and pictures can be helpful clues.

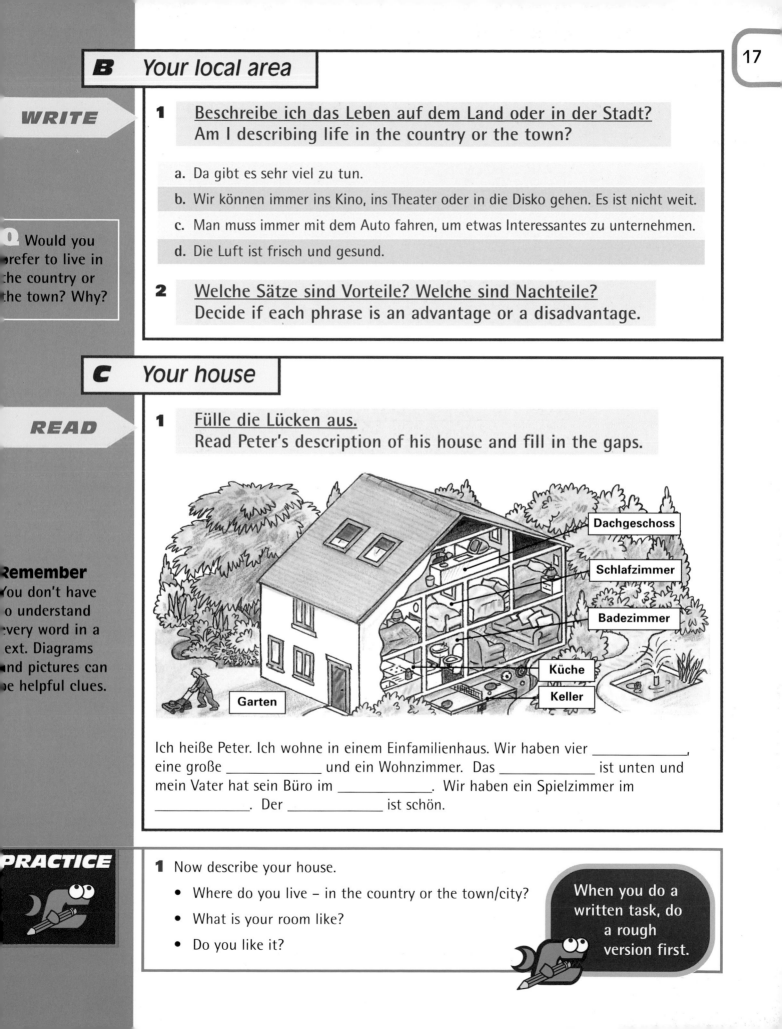

Dachgeschoss · Schlafzimmer · Badezimmer · Küche · Keller · Garten

Ich heiße Peter. Ich wohne in einem Einfamilienhaus. Wir haben vier _____, eine große _____ und ein Wohnzimmer. Das _____ ist unten und mein Vater hat sein Büro im _____. Wir haben ein Spielzimmer im _____. Der _____ ist schön.

PRACTICE

1 Now describe your house.
- Where do you live – in the country or the town/city?
- What is your room like?
- Do you like it?

When you do a written task, do a rough version first.

Vocabulary

A Interests and hobbies

Q Name the days of the week. Can you say you do a hobby every Monday?

Was für Hobbys hast du?		What are your hobbies?	
Meine Hobbys sind Sport/Kunst/Computer ...		My hobbies are sport/art/computers ...	
Ich schwimme/tanze/lese gern.		I like swimming/dancing/reading.	
Ich spiele gern Fußball/Volleyball ...		I like playing football/volleyball ...	
Was ist dein Lieblingssport?		What's your favourite sport?	
Mein Lieblingssport ist Squash/Hockey ...		My favourite sport is squash/hockey ...	
Tennis finde ich toll.		I think tennis is great.	
Ich fahre gern Rad/Skateboard ...		I like cycling/skateboarding ...	
Ich gehe gern ins Kino/Theater ...		I like going to the cinema/theatre ...	

angeln	to fish	der Federball/	
fotografieren	to photograph	Badminton	badminton
gewinnen	to win	die Ferien	holidays
hören	to hear/isten to	der Film	film
kegeln	to bowl	das Foto	photo
lesen	to read	der Fotoapparat	camera
Rad fahren	to cycle	das Freibad	open-air pool
reiten	to ride	der Fußball	football
sammeln	to collect	die Gitarre	guitar
Schlittschuh laufen	to skate	die Gymnastik	gymnastics
schwimmen	to swim	das Hallenbad	indoor pool
singen	to sing	der Jugendklub	youth club
Ski fahren	to ski	die Karten	cards
sparen	to save	die Musik	music
spazieren gehen	to go for a walk	das Rugby	rugby
spielen	to play	das Schach	chess
tanzen	to dance	das Stadion	stadium
wandern	to hike	das Tennis	tennis
die Briefmarke	stamps	das Theater	theatre
der Computer	computer	das Tischtennis	table tennis

Q What do you like to do in your spare time? Describe your typical weekend's entertainment.

B Home and local environment

Ich lebe in der Stadt/auf dem Land.		I live in the city/in the country.	
Es gibt ein Schloss/eine Kirche/einer Bahnhof.		There's a castle/a church / a station.	
Ich lebe lieber auf dem Land/in der Stadt.		I prefer living in the country/city.	
Es ist interessanter/nicht so hektisch.		It's more interesting/not so hectic.	

das Bett	bed	der Garten	garden
das Buch	book	das Haus	house
der Fernseher	television	die Küche	kitchen
die Kleider	clothes	das Schlafzimmer	bedroom
die Stereoanlage	stereo	das Spielzimmer	playroom
das Büro	office	das Wohnzimmer	living room

Remember
You can help yourself revise at home by naming everything you see around you in German.

Grammar

C The object (accusative) case

1 A simple sentence usually has a subject, verb and object.

- The subject does the action (I).
- The verb is the action (eat).
- The object has the action done to it (potatoes).

You (subject) are reading (verb) this book (object).

2 If a word with **the** or **a** in front is the subject of a sentence, the word for **the** or **a** does not change:

Der Mann ist groß.

Die Frau hat eine Katze.

Das Haus ist blau.

3 If it is the object of a sentence, the word for **the** or **a** changes only in the masculine:

Masculine object	Feminine object	Neuter object
Ich sehe **den** Mann.	Ich habe **die** Flasche.	Ich kaufe **das** Haus.
Ich sehe **einen** Mann.	Ich habe **eine** Flasche.	Ich kaufe **ein** Haus.

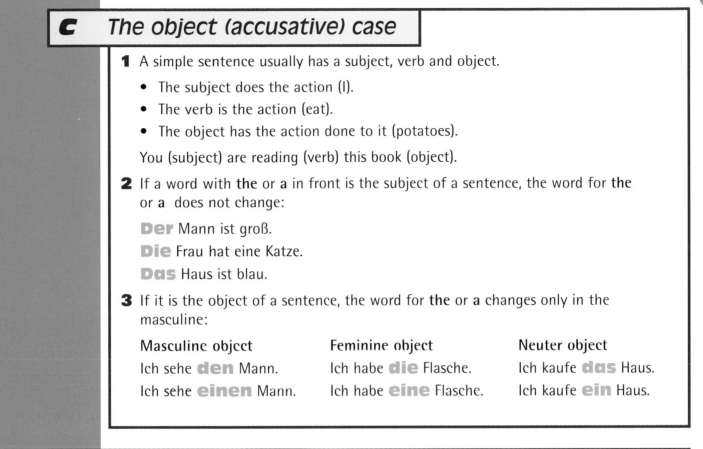

D Es gibt

1 When you are talking about what's in your town, you will probably use **es gibt**.

Es gibt ein Schloss. **Es gibt** einen Park.

2 The phrase **es gibt** is always followed by the object, which is also known as the **accusative case**. Do you remember the rules? Let's have a look.

Remember
Only the masculine changes!

	a/the	turns into	a/the (accusative case)
masculine	ein/der Bahnhof	→	Es gibt **einen/den** Bahnhof.
feminine	eine/der Kirche	→	Es gibt **eine/der** Kirche.
neuter	ein/das Stadion	→	Es gibt **ein/das** Stadion.
plural	Autos	→	Es gibt Autos.

Q Use es gibt to say what there is/are in your town.

3 The adjective endings change too:

Es gibt ein**en** groß**en** Bahnhof/ein**e** alt**e** Kirche/ein schön**es** Stadion.

Daily routine

THE BARE BONES

➤ You need to be able to talk about, write about and recognise information about your daily routine for the exam.

➤ Make sure you can tell the time and talk about how long something takes.

A Travel to school

SPEAK

1 <u>Was passt zusammen? Lies die Sätze vor.</u>
Match the phrases to the pictures. Say them aloud.

Q How do you get to school? How long does it take?

a Ich fahre mit dem Zug.

b Ich fahre mit dem Bus.

c Ich fahre mit dem Fahrrad.

d Ich gehe zu Fuß.

1 30 min

2 10 min

3 45 min

4 20 min

e Die Fahrt dauert fünfundvierzig Minuten.

f Die Fahrt dauert zwanzig Minuten.

g Die Fahrt dauert eine halbe Stunde.

h Die Fahrt dauert zehn Minuten.

B School subjects

WRITE

1 <u>Fülle die Lücken mit den richtigen Fächern aus.</u>
Fill in the timetable with the correct subject.

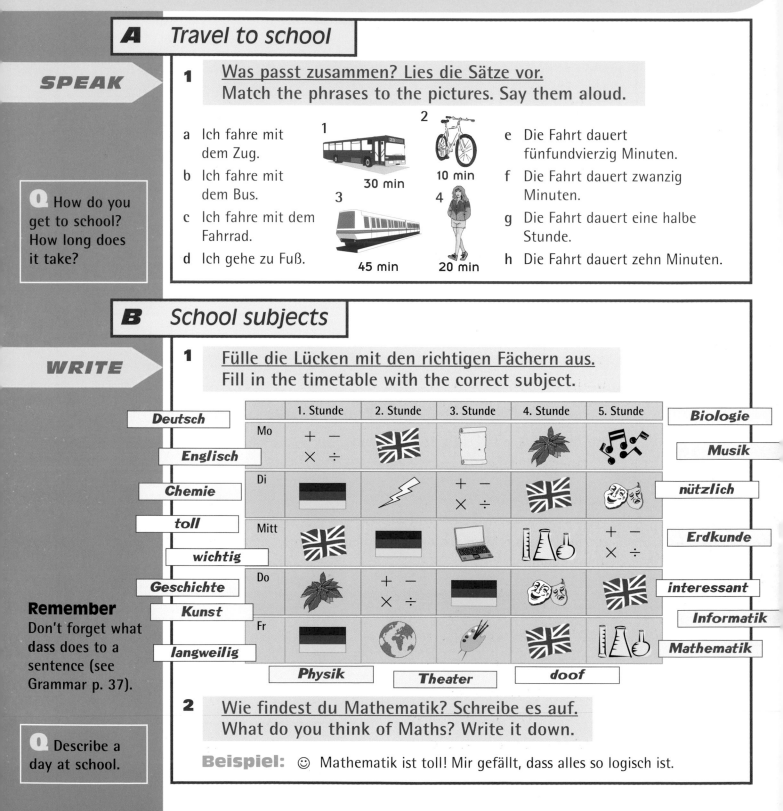

Deutsch • Englisch • Chemie • toll • wichtig • Geschichte • Kunst • langweilig

Biologie • Musik • nützlich • Erdkunde • interessant • Informatik • Mathematik

Physik • Theater • doof

	1. Stunde	2. Stunde	3. Stunde	4. Stunde	5. Stunde
Mo	+ − × ÷				
Di			+ − × ÷		
Mitt					+ − × ÷
Do		+ − × ÷			
Fr					

Remember
Don't forget what *dass* does to a sentence (see Grammar p. 37).

Q Describe a day at school.

2 <u>Wie findest du Mathematik? Schreibe es auf.</u>
What do you think of Maths? Write it down.

Beispiel: ☺ Mathematik ist toll! Mir gefällt, dass alles so logisch ist.

C School routine

READ

1 <u>Gerd spricht über seinen Schultag. Lies den Text.</u>
Gerd is speaking about his school day. Read the text.

Remember
Halb elf does NOT mean half past eleven. What does it mean?

Ich wache um zehn vor sieben auf. Fünf Minuten später stehe ich auf. Ich muss vor sieben Uhr duschen. Der Schulbus fährt um Viertel nach sieben ab. Die Bushaltestelle ist gerade vor meiner Haustür. Die Fahrt dauert eine Viertelstunde.

Um halb acht bin ich schon auf dem Schulhof. Ich rede mit meinen Freunden und der Unterricht beginnt um Viertel vor acht. Wir haben um halb elf eine kleine Pause, in der man etwas trinken oder einen kleinen Snack essen kann.

Die Mittagspause beginnt um zwölf Uhr und dauert eine dreiviertel Stunde. Um Viertel vor eins haben wir noch Unterricht. Die Schule ist erst um vierzehn Uhr aus.

2 <u>Beantworte die Fragen.</u>
Answer the questions.

a Wann steht Gerd auf?

b Um wieviel Uhr fährt der Schulbus ab?

c Wie lange dauert die Fahrt zur Schule?

d Um wieviel Uhr ist die Mittagspause?

e Wann ist die Schule aus?

Q Describe your typical school day from the moment you wake up. How is your daily routine different at the weekends?

PRACTICE

1 Imagine you are Madonna or Robbie Williams. Describe your daily routine. Think about:

- what time you get up
- when you have breakfast
- how and where you go to work
- what you eat for lunch and at what time
- when you come home
- what you do in the evening
- what time you go to bed.

In the speaking exam, if you think of questions you want to ask, ask them, just like you would in a normal conversation!

School and future plans

THE BARE BONES

➤ You'll need to be able to understand instructions, both in the classroom and in the exam.

➤ Be prepared to describe your school and talk about your favourite subjects.

➤ When talking about what you want to do after school, you'll need the future tense.

A Classroom instructions

WRITE

1 Ordne die Sätze!
Put the instructions in order.

a Fragen die Beantworte

b Mache Dialog einen

c auf die Details Schreibe

d Information Gib über

e Finde passenden Bilder die

Q How many classroom/exam instructions can you remember?

2 Schreibe die Sätze auf Englisch.
Translate the instructions into English.

B About my school

READ

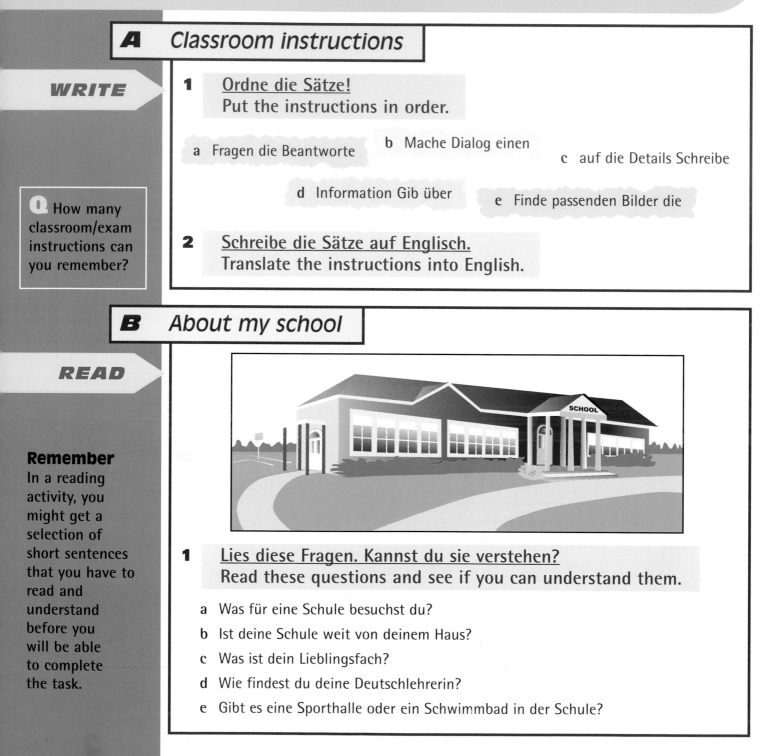

Remember
In a reading activity, you might get a selection of short sentences that you have to read and understand before you will be able to complete the task.

1 Lies diese Fragen. Kannst du sie verstehen?
Read these questions and see if you can understand them.

a Was für eine Schule besuchst du?

b Ist deine Schule weit von deinem Haus?

c Was ist dein Lieblingsfach?

d Wie findest du deine Deutschlehrerin?

e Gibt es eine Sporthalle oder ein Schwimmbad in der Schule?

B

Q What do you really like about school and why? Write a hundred words. Remember to use weil: 'Ich liebe die Schule, weil meine Freunde da sind'.

2 <u>Was passt zusammen?</u>
Match the questions from 1 with the correct answers.

1 Mathe. [c]

2 Sie ist einen Kilometer von meinem Haus entfernt. [ ]

3 Sie ist sehr intelligent, aber manchmal ein bisschen langweilig. [ ]

4 Beides, wir haben eine Sporthalle und ein Schwimmbad. [ ]

5 Die Schule ist ein Gymnasium. [ ]

C Future plans

WRITE

1 <u>Unterstreiche die nützlichen Wörter und Sätze in diesem Text.</u>
Which words or phrases in this text might be useful for writing your own version? Underline them.

Remember
In the exam, even for a writing task, you will probably need to do some reading. If you are given a model text, be sure to use it.

> Ich heiße Michael Franz. Ich wohne in Karlsruhe und besuche das Gymnasium in Wörth. Es gibt im Moment viel zu tun an der Schule, das gefällt mir. Ich mag es nicht, gelangweilt zu sein. Nach meinen Prüfungen habe ich vor nach Amerika zu fahren. Ich werde da für Camp Amerika mit den Kindern arbeiten. Ich möchte auch ein bisschen durch das Land fahren. Ich interessiere mich sehr für die Vereinigten Staaten.

2 <u>Jetzt schreibe deinen eigenen Text.</u>
Write your own text, using the words you underlined.

PRACTICE

1 Schreibe einen Brief an deinen Brieffreund.

Beschreibe:

• deine Schule – wo sie ist, was für eine Schule, dein Lieblingsfach und deinen Lieblingslehrer/deine Lieblingslehrerin und warum

• was dir im Moment gefällt

• was dir nicht gefällt

• was du im Sommer machen möchtest.

Any information you are given in the exam can be used to help you. Underline any parts you think are important. Be sure to read the task carefully first.

Vocabulary

A Daily routine

Wie kommst du zur Schule?	*How do you get to school?*
Ich fahre mit dem Bus/Zug/Auto.	*I travel by bus/train/car.*
Ich bin mit dem Auto gefahren.	*I came by car.*
Ich gehe zu Fuß.	*I walk.*
Die Fahrt dauert eine halbe Stunde.	*The journey lasts half an hour.*
Wann beginnt die Schule?	*When does school begin?*
Wann ist die Schule aus?	*When does school end?*
Ich habe jeden Abend zwei Stunden Hausaufgaben.	*I have two hours' homework every night*
Wann stehst du auf?	*When do you get up?*

Biologie	*Biology*	Mathematik	*Maths*
Chemie	*Chemistry*	Musik	*Music*
Deutsch	*German*	Kunst	*Art*
Englisch	*English*	Naturwissenschaften	*Science*
Erdkunde	*Geography*	Physik	*Physics*
Geschichte	*History*	Theater	*Drama*
Informatik	*IT*		

doof	*stupid*	nützlich	*useful*
interessant	*interesting*	toll	*great*
langweilig	*boring*	wichtig	*important*

Q Write three sentences about each school subject. Say what you think of it and why. Give any other information you can.

B School and future plans

Hör gut zu.	*Listen.*
Beantworte die Fragen.	*Answer the questions.*
Lies die Sätze.	*Read the sentences.*
Mache Notizen.	*Make notes.*
Schreibe die passenden Wörter auf.	*Write the correct words.*
Ich mag Deutsch/Englisch/Französisch ...	*I like German/English/French ...*
Mein Lieblingsfach ist Mathe/Religion/Kunst ...	*My favourite subject is Maths/RE/Art ...*
Meine Lieblingsfächer sind Sport und Kunst.	*My favourite subjects are Sport and Art.*
Geschichte mag ich am liebsten.	*I like History best of all.*
Ich mag Physik (gar) nicht.	*I don't like Physics (at all).*
Ich hasse Erdkunde.	*I hate Geography.*
Wie bitte?	*Pardon?*
Wiederholen Sie, bitte.	*Please repeat that.*
Langsamer, bitte.	*Slower, please.*
Ich verstehe nicht.	*I don't understand.*
Was für eine Schule besuchst du?	*What sort of school do you go to?*
Sie ist einen Kilometer von meinem Haus entfernt.	*It's 1km away from my house.*

Grammar

C The future tense

There are two ways of making the future tense, both are easy! Do you remember them?

1 Use words which indicate you are talking about the future + the present tense!
For example:

Morgen		I will travel to London
Nächste Woche	+ **fahre ich** nach London. =	tomorrow
Samstag		next week
		on Saturday.

2 Use **werden** + infinitive.

ich	werde
du	wirst
er/sie/es	wird
wir	werden
ihr	werdet
Sie/sie	werden

Ich **werde** nach London **fahren**. = I **will** travel to London.

> **Q** Describe what you are going to do tomorrow.

D Man kann ... + infinitive

1 This is a very useful way of describing possible activities.

Was **kann man** nach der Schule **machen**?

Man kann	eine Theater-AG **machen**.
	Handball **spielen**.
	schwimmen **gehen**.
	mit Freunden **ausgehen**.

> **Q** Practise using this construction – it sounds really authentic!

> Remember, the exam is a chance for you to show off what you can do. Learn some impressive-sounding sentences and phrases and then make sure you use them!

Travel, transport and directions

THE BARE BONES

➤ Being able to describe your local area, your town and places in it can be useful in various parts of the exam.

➤ Giving and understanding directions regularly feature in exam questions.

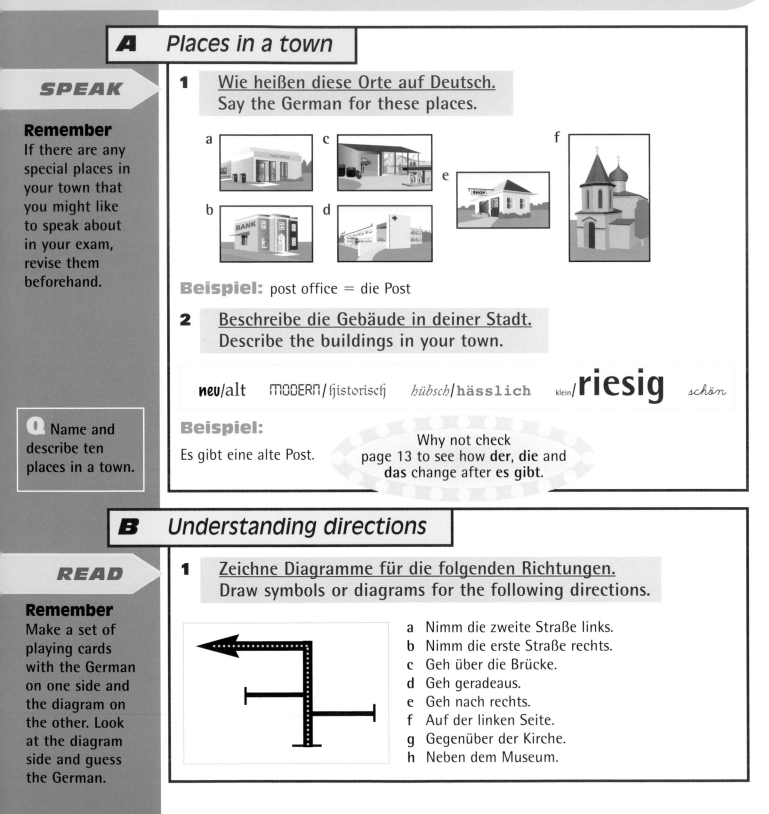

A Places in a town

SPEAK

Remember
If there are any special places in your town that you might like to speak about in your exam, revise them beforehand.

1 <u>Wie heißen diese Orte auf Deutsch.</u>
Say the German for these places.

a

c

f

b

d

e

Beispiel: post office = die Post

2 <u>Beschreibe die Gebäude in deiner Stadt.</u>
Describe the buildings in your town.

neu/alt   MODERN/historisch   hübsch/hässlich   klein/**riesig**   schön

Beispiel:

Es gibt eine alte Post.

*Why not check page 13 to see how **der, die** and **das** change after **es gibt**.*

Q Name and describe ten places in a town.

B Understanding directions

READ

Remember
Make a set of playing cards with the German on one side and the diagram on the other. Look at the diagram side and guess the German.

1 <u>Zeichne Diagramme für die folgenden Richtungen.</u>
Draw symbols or diagrams for the following directions.

a Nimm die zweite Straße links.
b Nimm die erste Straße rechts.
c Geh über die Brücke.
d Geh geradeaus.
e Geh nach rechts.
f Auf der linken Seite.
g Gegenüber der Kirche.
h Neben dem Museum.

C Giving directions

Remember
Do some rough notes first to be sure of what you are going to write. Give as much information as you can.

1 <u>Schreibe die Richtungen auf von der Bushaltestelle zu deinem Haus.</u>
Write down the directions from the bus stop to your house.

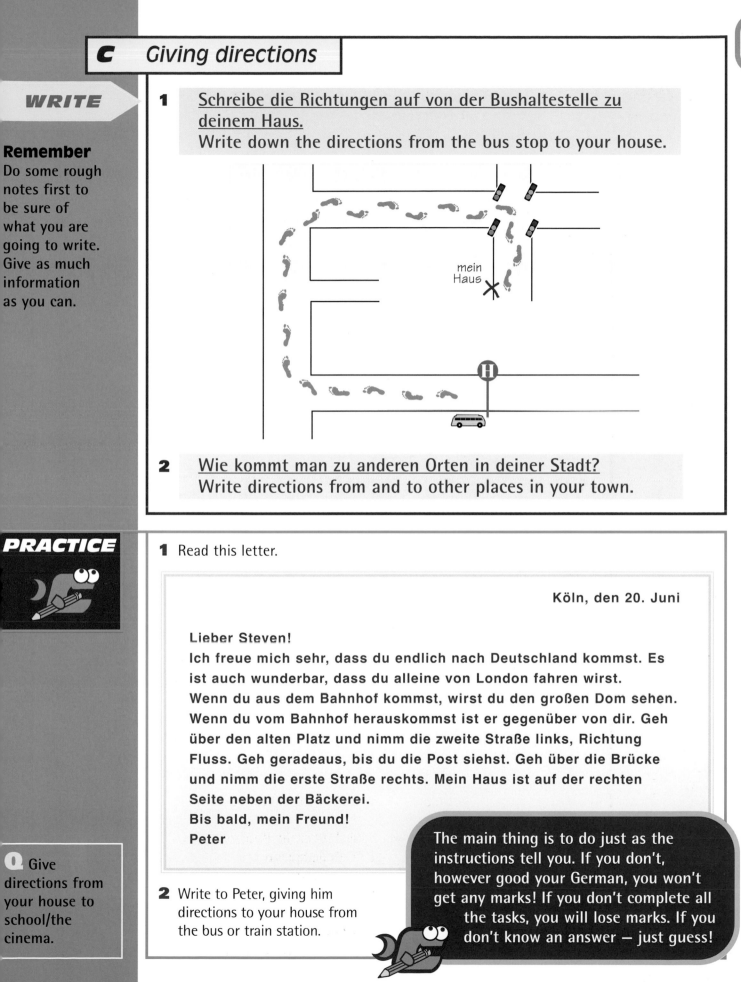

2 <u>Wie kommt man zu anderen Orten in deiner Stadt?</u>
Write directions from and to other places in your town.

1 Read this letter.

Köln, den 20. Juni

Lieber Steven!
Ich freue mich sehr, dass du endlich nach Deutschland kommst. Es ist auch wunderbar, dass du alleine von London fahren wirst.
Wenn du aus dem Bahnhof kommst, wirst du den großen Dom sehen. Wenn du vom Bahnhof herauskommst ist er gegenüber von dir. Geh über den alten Platz und nimm die zweite Straße links, Richtung Fluss. Geh geradeaus, bis du die Post siehst. Geh über die Brücke und nimm die erste Straße rechts. Mein Haus ist auf der rechten Seite neben der Bäckerei.
Bis bald, mein Freund!
Peter

Q Give directions from your house to school/the cinema.

2 Write to Peter, giving him directions to your house from the bus or train station.

The main thing is to do just as the instructions tell you. If you don't, however good your German, you won't get any marks! If you don't complete all the tasks, you will lose marks. If you don't know an answer — just guess!

THE BARE BONES

➤ Giving information about yourself is relevant to most activities in the exam. It's also useful for this topic.

➤ Talking about your holidays can be a safe way of using all three tenses and expressing opinion.

A Getting tourist information

SPEAK

1 Lies diese E-Mail.
Read this e-mail to the Berlin tourist office.

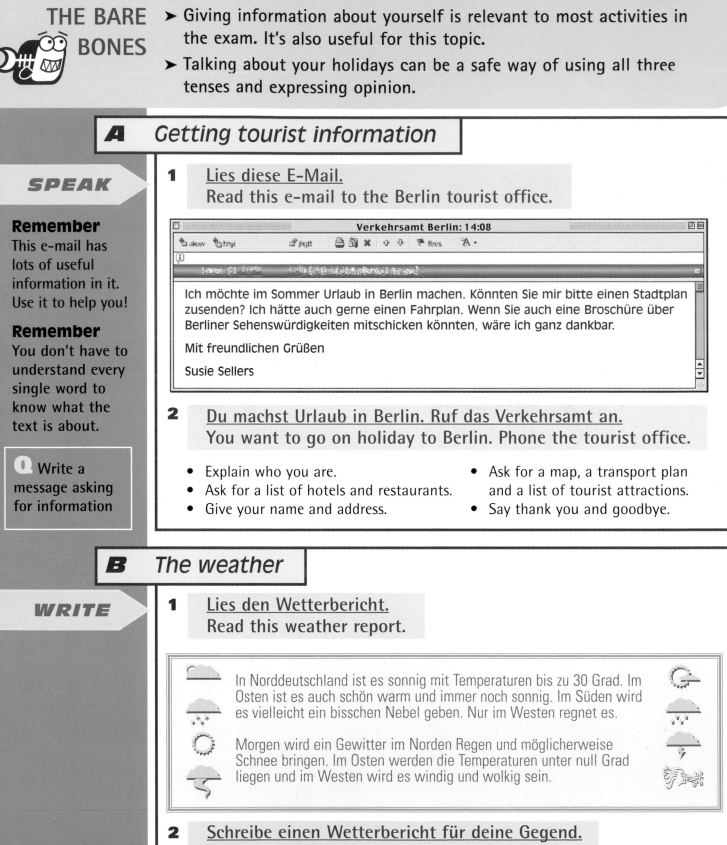

Verkehrsamt Berlin: 14:08

Ich möchte im Sommer Urlaub in Berlin machen. Könnten Sie mir bitte einen Stadtplan zusenden? Ich hätte auch gerne einen Fahrplan. Wenn Sie auch eine Broschüre über Berliner Sehenswürdigkeiten mitschicken könnten, wäre ich ganz dankbar.

Mit freundlichen Grüßen

Susie Sellers

Remember
This e-mail has lots of useful information in it. Use it to help you!

Remember
You don't have to understand every single word to know what the text is about.

Q Write a message asking for information

2 Du machst Urlaub in Berlin. Ruf das Verkehrsamt an.
You want to go on holiday to Berlin. Phone the tourist office.

- Explain who you are.
- Ask for a list of hotels and restaurants.
- Give your name and address.
- Ask for a map, a transport plan and a list of tourist attractions.
- Say thank you and goodbye.

B The weather

WRITE

1 Lies den Wetterbericht.
Read this weather report.

In Norddeutschland ist es sonnig mit Temperaturen bis zu 30 Grad. Im Osten ist es auch schön warm und immer noch sonnig. Im Süden wird es vielleicht ein bisschen Nebel geben. Nur im Westen regnet es.

Morgen wird ein Gewitter im Norden Regen und möglicherweise Schnee bringen. Im Osten werden die Temperaturen unter null Grad liegen und im Westen wird es windig und wolkig sein.

2 Schreibe einen Wetterbericht für deine Gegend.
Write a weather forecast for where you live.

C Different holidays

READ

1 <u>Welche Person passt zu welcher Urlaubsreklame?</u>
Which person fits which holiday ad?

Remember
Sometimes there are more answers to choose from than questions in the exam. Don't let this put you off!

Q What sort of holiday would you love to go on?

PRACTICE

1

Lanzarote…

… wo die Sonne immer scheint. Sonnen Sie sich an unseren schönen sandigen Stränden und entspannen Sie sich. Hier ist der Urlaub langsam, leise und warm.

> Im Urlaub möchte ich am Strand schlafen, Romane lesen und im Salzwasser schwimmen.

Ulrich

> Ich zelte gern und möchte lange Wanderungen unternehmen. Ich liebe die Natur.

Markus

> Als Familie gefällt es uns, in der Stadt Urlaub zu machen. Wir schauen uns gerne Museen, historische Gebäude und weltberühmte Sehenswürdigkeiten an.

Gerthrud

2

Aktiv in der Türkei

Kommen Sie in die Türkei und genießen Sie unsere tolle Küste. Mit einem Gulet können Sie auf dem Wasser leben, sich entspannen und die Türkei entdecken.

3

Großbritannien

Geschichte, Geschichte und noch mehr Geschichte! Wenn Sie sich für historisches Geschehen, alte Gebäude und Geschichten voller Geschichte interessieren, fliegen Sie direkt nach London für die Erfahrung des Lebens.

4

BODENSEE CAMPINGPLATZ

Neben dem Wasser, tolles Wetter, schöne Landschaft, moderne Unterkunft, nicht teuer.

---

1 Record a holiday message to send to a friend. Tell him:

- where you are

- who you are with

- how long you are staying for

- what the weather is like

- what activities you have been doing.

> In the speaking exam, you are allowed to prepare what you are going to say and make notes before you go in. Practise making notes and speaking from them.

Vocabulary

A Travel, transport and directions

Entschuldigen Sie, bitte.	*Excuse me please.*
Wo ist hier eine Toilette?	*Where is there a toilet near here?*
Wo ist die nächste Bushaltestelle?	*Where is the nearest bus stop?*
Sie gehen geradeaus.	*Go straight ahead.*
Ist es weit?	*Is it far?*
Das ist nur fünf Minuten von hier zu Fuß.	*It's only five minutes' walk from here.*
Das ist hier in der Nähe.	*It's nearby.*
Entschuldigen Sie bitte, können Sie mir helfen?	*Excuse me please, can you help me?*
Wo ist ...?	*Where is ...?*
Wie komme ich am besten zum/zur ...?	*What's the best way to get to ...?*
Ich suche die Hauptstraße/den Bahnhof.	*I'm looking for the High Street/station.*
Nehmen Sie die erste/zweite Straße links/rechts.	*Take the 1st/2nd on the left/right.*
Gehen Sie geradeaus.	*Go straight on.*

der Bahnhof	*station*	die Sehenswürdigkeit	*sight, something worth seeing*
das Einkaufszentrum	*shopping centre*		
das Gasthaus	*hotel*	das Sportzentrum	*sports centre*
die Geschäfte	*shops*	der Zoo	*zoo*
die Kirche	*church*	hässlich	*ugly*
das Krankenhaus	*hospital*	hübsch	*pretty*
der Markt	*market*	klein	*small*
das Rathaus	*town hall*	riesig	*enormous*
das Schloss	*castle*		

Q Give directions for how to get to school from your house.

B Tourism

Ich zelte gern.	*I like camping.*
Es gefällt mir, in der Stadt Urlaub zu machen.	*I like to holiday in the town.*
Ich interessiere mich für Kultur.	*I am interested in culture.*
Es ist eine mittelgroße Stadt.	*It's a medium-sized town.*
Die Gegend ist herrlich.	*The area is lovely.*
Wie wird das Wetter morgen?	*What will the weather be like tomorrow?*
Wie ist die Wettervorhersage?	*What's the weather forecast?*
Am Vormittag wird es kalt sein.	*It's going to be cold in the morning.*
In der Nacht wird es schneien.	*It's going to snow in the night.*
Im Herbst ist es oft nebelig.	*It's often foggy in autumn.*
Es donnert und blitzt.	*There's thunder and lightning.*

die Broschüre	*brochure*	Es friert.	*It's freezing.*
der Fahrplan	*transport plan*	Es ist wolkig.	*It's cloudy.*
der Stadtplan	*town plan*	Es ist nebelig.	*It's foggy.*
das Verkehrsamt	*tourist office*	Es ist windig.	*It's windy.*
Es regnet.	*It's raining.*	Es ist warm.	*It's warm.*
Es schneit.	*It's snowing.*	Es ist kalt.	*It's cold.*
Es blitzt.	*There's lightning.*	Es gibt ein Gewitter.	*There's a storm.*

C Saying how you feel about something

1 Adverbs add extra information to a verb. In German, the adverb is exactly the same as the adjective:

langsam = slow <u>and</u> slowly

2 Adverbs are usually placed after the verb they describe:

Du läufst **schnell**. You can run fast.

3 You can use the adverb **gern** to show that you like something:

Hast du Schokolade **gern**? Do you like chocolate?

Ich sehe **gern** fern. I like watching TV.

4 Add **sehr** to say you really like something:

Ich lese **sehr** gern Bücher. I really like reading books.

5 Add **nicht** to say you don't like something:

Ich studiere **nicht gern** Mathematik. I don't like studying Maths.

6 Use **lieber** to say you prefer doing something:

Ich gehe **lieber** schwimmen. I prefer to go swimming.

D Time

1 To find out the time, you ask the question **Wieviel Uhr ist es?**

2 For 'o'clock', you just use the numbers one to twelve followed by the word **Uhr**.

Es ist zehn Uhr. It's ten o'clock.

3 If you want to say something is happening **at** a certain time, you use the word **um**.

Die Schule beginnt **um** acht Uhr. Ich stehe **um** sieben Uhr auf.

4 For minutes past the hour, you use the word **nach**.

Es ist fünf **nach** elf. Es ist Viertel **nach** elf.

5 For minutes to the hour, you use the word **vor**.

Es ist fünfundzwanzig **vor** zwölf. Es ist Viertel **vor** zwölf.

6 In German you don't say 'half past', like in English. You say 'half to' the next hour.

Es ist **halb zwölf**. = It's half past eleven.

7 When you talk about the times of buses, coaches, trains or other transport, you use the 24-hour clock in German.

Der Zug fährt um **zwanzig Uhr dreißig** ab.

The train leaves at 8.30pm.

8 Remember that **Uhr** only means 'o'clock' and 'clock'. The word for an hour (sixty minutes) is **die Stunde**.

Accommodation

THE BARE BONES

➤ Booking hotels is likely to come up in the exam. Make sure you know what to say and do.

➤ Whether it's writing to book a room or complaining about a problem, you should be able to do it confidently and correctly.

A Booking a room

READ

1 <u>Lies die Briefe.</u>
Read the letters.

Frankfurt, den 16. Mai

Lieber Herbergsvater!
Ich habe vor nach Bad Marienberg zu fahren. Ich möchte drei Nächte vom 5. bis zum 8. Juli bei Ihnen in der Jugendherberge bleiben. Haben Sie Plätze frei? Ich lege eine frankierte Postkarte für Ihre Antwort bei.

Vielen Dank im Voraus.

Ihr
Max Tintern

Guildford, den 15. Juli

Lieber Herbergsvater!
Im Sommer habe ich vor mit drei Freunden und zwei Freundinnen nach Freiburg zu fahren. Wir möchten eine Nacht bei Ihnen in Recklinghausen am 27. August übernachten. Ich rufe nächste Woche an, um die Reservierung zu bestätigen.

Vielen Dank, mit bestem Gruß,

Susanna Van Swaay

---

a Wer hat vor, eine Nacht in der Jugendherberge zu verbringen?

b Wieviele Personen gibt es insgesamt in der Gruppe von Susanna?

c Wo sind die zwei Jugendherbergen?

d Was legt Max in seinem Brief bei?

e Wann hat Susanna vor, in die Jugendherberge zu kommen?

Q Write a letter to a hotel or youth hostel to book a room.

B Accommodation facilities

WRITE

1 <u>Wo im Hotel ist ...?</u>
Where are these things in your imaginary hotel?

a) restaurant   b) swimming pool   c) bedrooms with a bath   d) car park   e) lounge

Beispiel: Das Restaurant ist im Erdgeschoss.

Q Give information about:
• mealtimes
• lifts or stairs
• other facilities.

C Problems

SPEAK

1 <u>Verbinde die Probleme mit den möglichen Entschuldigungen.</u>
Match the problems with the possible responses.

a
😞
Die Dusche in meinem Zimmer funktioniert nicht.

1
😊
Ich organisiere für Sie sofort ein anderes Zimmer.

b
😞
Es ist zu warm im Zimmer.

2
😊
Wir bringen Ihnen sofort noch eins.

c
😞
Der Lärm von der Disko ist zu laut.

3
😊
Ich kann die Heizung direkt ausschalten/anschalten.

d
😞
Mein Getränk ist warm, Bier schmeckt nicht gut so.

4
😊
Ich schicke einen Mechaniker nach oben zu Ihnen.

2 <u>Mache Dialoge.</u>
Make up dialogues for the situations above.

PRACTICE

1 Telephone a hotel in Austria to book a room for your holiday.

You would like a double room with bath from 3 to 7 July.

- Give your name and spell it.
- Give your address, spell it if necessary.
- Give your telephone number.

Ask for the full address of the hotel and write it down.

In the exam, the number of marks for each answer is given in brackets. This will help you to decide how much time to spend on each question.

Eating out

THE BARE BONES

➤ Talking about eating out gives you another opportunity to express opinions and use more than one tense.

➤ Make sure you know all the right vocabulary and be prepared to show it off!

A Where do you want to eat?

READ

1 <u>Sieh diese Schilder an.</u>
Look at these signs.

Remember
In the exam, you might get signs and posters to read. Look for key words and use any clues (e.g. pictures, words which are like English).

Q Which of these eating places would you like to go to? Why?

IMBISSSTUBE

CURRYWURST €3,-

HAMBURGER €2,20

POMMES €1,50

KARTOFFELSALAT €2,50

═══════

ÖFFNUNGSZEITEN VON
11 UHR BIS 21 UHR.

Café Callista

Frühstück
Kaffee und Kuchen
Bier und Wein
Kleine Gerichte

Täglich geöffnet
10:00–24:00

Topo Gigio

Italienische

Spezialitäten

Pizza, Pasta,

Eis und Bier

Öffnungsz.:

tägl. 12–23 Uhr

2 <u>Ist das richtig oder falsch? Schreibe die Sätze richtig auf.</u>
True or false? Write the sentences out correctly.

a Topo Gigio ist ein japanisches Restaurant.
b Café Callista ist am Montag geschlossen.
c Pizza ist eine italienische Spezialität.
d In der Imbissstube kann man nur Pommes essen.

B What would you like to eat?

SPEAK

1 <u>Ordne die Sätze in der richtigen Reihenfolge.</u>
Put the sentences in the correct order.

1 HERR SCHMIDT: Danke ... Ich nehme ein Steak mit Salat und ein Glas Rotwein, bitte.
2 KELLNER: Möchten Sie sonst noch etwas?
3 KELLNER: Ach ja, Herr Schmidt, bitte, Ihr Tisch ... Hier ist die Speisekarte.
4 HERR SCHMIDT: Ja danke, das war wirklich lecker!
5 HERR SCHMIDT: Guten Tag, mein Name ist Schmidt, ich habe eine Reservierung für acht Uhr.
6 KELLNER: (einbisschen später) Bitte, Ihr Steak, und ... die Getränke. Guten Appetit! (ein bisschen später) Hat's geschmeckt?
7 HERR SCHMIDT: Nein danke, die Rechnung nur.

B

2   <u>Mache einen Dialog.</u>
Make up a dialogue for the following situation.

> Reservierung: 19:30; 2 Personen
> Essen: zweimal Hähnchen und Salat
> Getränke: ein Glas Weißwein,
> ein Bier und eine große Flasche
> Mineralwasser
> Problem: Der Wein ist warm.

Q Write the script for a conversation in a restaurant. Make sure there is a problem for one of the diners!

C   Opinions about food

WRITE

1   <u>Stelle eine Liste auf.</u>
Write a list of foods that you like and don't like.

Ich esse gern ...   Ich esse nicht gern ...

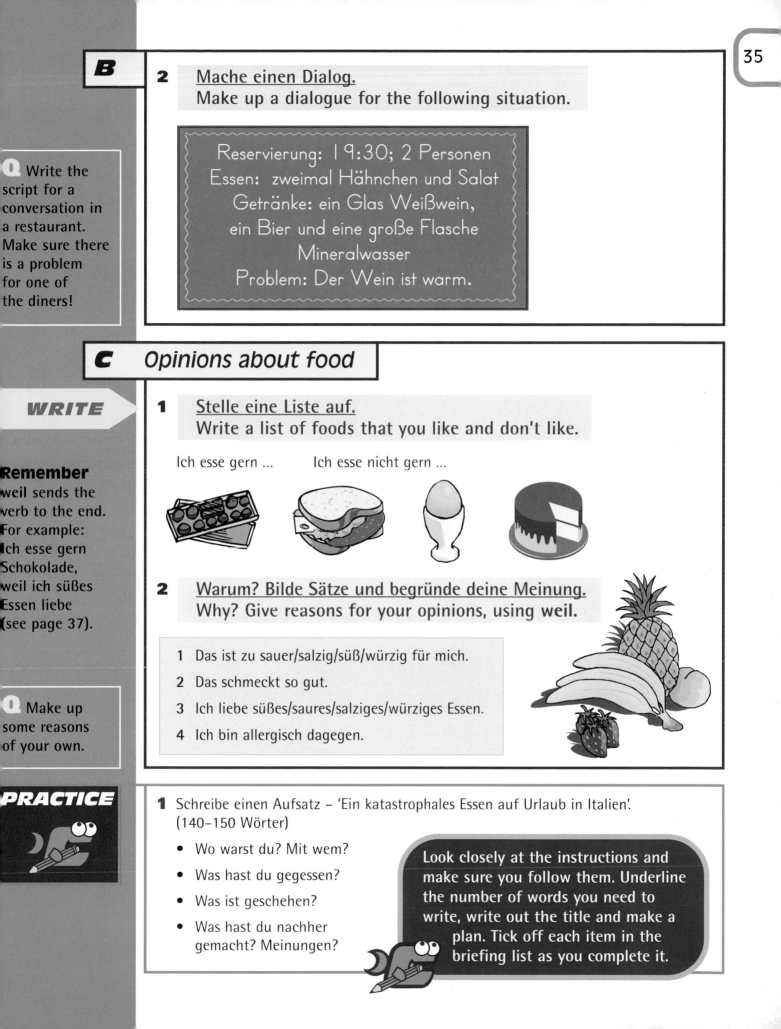

Remember
weil sends the verb to the end. For example:
Ich esse gern Schokolade, weil ich süßes Essen liebe (see page 37).

2   <u>Warum? Bilde Sätze und begründe deine Meinung.</u>
Why? Give reasons for your opinions, using weil.

1   Das ist zu sauer/salzig/süß/würzig für mich.
2   Das schmeckt so gut.
3   Ich liebe süßes/saures/salziges/würziges Essen.
4   Ich bin allergisch dagegen.

Q Make up some reasons of your own.

PRACTICE

1   Schreibe einen Aufsatz – 'Ein katastrophales Essen auf Urlaub in Italien'.
(140–150 Wörter)

● Wo warst du? Mit wem?

● Was hast du gegessen?

● Was ist geschehen?

● Was hast du nachher gemacht? Meinungen?

Look closely at the instructions and make sure you follow them. Underline the number of words you need to write, write out the title and make a plan. Tick off each item in the briefing list as you complete it.

Vocabulary

A Accommodation

Haben Sie ein Zimmer für heute Nacht?	Have you got a room for tonight?
Haben Sie Platz für zwei Personen?	Have you got room for two people?
Ich möchte ein Doppelzimmer mit Bad.	I'd like a double room with a bath.
Was kostet ein Zimmer mit Dusche?	What does a room with a shower cost?
Ich nehme das Zimmer.	I'll take the room.
Gibt es einen Parkplatz?	Is there a car park?
Wann ist Frühstück?	When is breakfast?
Was kostet eine Übernachtung?	What does overnight accommodation cost?

das Doppelzimmer	double room	die Jugendherberge	youth hostel
das Einzelzimmer	single room	die Rechnung	bill
im Erdgeschoss	on the ground floor	reservieren	to reserve
im Untergeschoss	on the lower ground floor	der Schlüssel	key
		die Übernachtung	overnight stay
im ersten Stock	on the first floor	im Untergeschoss	in the basement
die Halbpension	half board		

B Eating out

Die Speisekarte bitte.	The menu please.
Sonst noch etwas?	Anything else?
Ich habe eine Reservierung für acht Uhr.	I have a reservation for 8.00pm.
Das war wirklich lecker!	That was really tasty!
Ich nehme ein Steak mit Kartoffelsalat.	I would like steak with potato salad.
Ich esse gern Zwiebeln.	I like onions.
Ich esse nicht gern Champignons.	I don't like mushrooms.
Ich möchte ein Glas Mineralwasser.	I'd like a glass of mineral water.
Als Nachtisch hätte ich gern ein Eis.	For dessert, I'd like an ice cream.
Was für Eis haben Sie?	What sort of ice cream do you have?
Die Torte war besonders gut!	The gateau was particularly good.
Entschuldigen Sie, wo sind hier die Toiletten?	Excuse me, where are the toilets?
Zahlen, bitte.	The bill, please.
Was macht das, bitte?	What does that come to, please?
Herr Ober!	Waiter!
Zweimal Hähnchen mit Pommes.	Two chicken with chips.

geschlossen	shut	das Bier	beer
geöffnet	open	das Brot	bread
lecker	tasty	das Brötchen	bread roll
scharf	spicy	das Ei	egg
süß	sweet	das Eis	ice cream
der Apfel	apple	die Gabel	fork
der Apfelsaft	apple juice	das Hähnchen	chicken

B

der Joghurt	*yoghurt*	der Schinken	*ham*
die Kartoffel	*potato*	die Schokolade	*chocolate*
der Käse	*cheese*	der Senf	*mustard*
die Limonade	*lemonade*	das Spiegelei	*fried egg*
der Löffel	*spoon*	die Tasse	*cup*
das Menü	*fixed price menu*	der Tee	*tea*
das Messer	*knife*	der Wein	*wine*
das Mineralwasser	*mineral water*	die Wurst	*sausage*
der Orangensaft	*orange juice*	der Zucker	*sugar*
der Pfeffer	*pepper*	essen	*to eat*
die Sahne	*cream*	schmecken	*to taste*
das Salz	*salt*	trinken	*to drink*

Grammar

C Plurals

Q Find the singular and plural forms of these nouns: egg, bread roll, cup, sausage, apple, banana.

1 As well as knowing whether words are **der, die** or **das**, it's important to know how to make them plural too. In German, plurals are made in different ways. In dictionaries you find the plural before the English translation:

Bild das; -*er*   die Bilder
Buch das; *Bücher*   die Bücher
Landkarte die; -*n*   die Landkarten
Schreibtisch der; -*e*   die Schreibtische
Zimmer das; -   die Zimmer

2 It's a good idea to learn new nouns with their plural form as well.

D Weil

Q Join these sentences using weil.

Ich mag Köln. Die Stadt ist schön.

Ich habe eine Katze. Ich liebe Tiere.

1 When you were describing what food you like to eat and why in this section, you had to use the word **weil**. (Remember there's always a comma before it.)

Ich esse gern Schokolade, **weil** ich süßes Essen **liebe**!

2 Do you remember what the word **weil** does to a sentence? It sends the verb to the end! The word **dass** also sends the verb to the end.

Every time you make a statement in German, try to justify it with a 'because'. If you get in the habit of doing this, it will come more naturally in the exam.

Services

THE BARE BONES

➤ Situations in post offices, banks, lost-property offices and other places are often the subject for the speaking exam.

➤ Using polite forms and being able to communicate clearly are important skills.

➤ Be sure you know high numbers for the money exchange.

A Services

READ

1 Welches Geschlecht haben diese Wörter?
What is the gender – **der, die** or **das**?

a _____ Post   c _____ Geldautomat   e _____ Telefonzelle

b _____ Fundbüro   d _____ Apotheke   f _____ Fahrradverleih

Remember
You can always check genders in the Vocabulary section.

2 Verbinde die Wörter mit den richtigen Beschreibungen.
Now match the places with the descriptions of what you can do there.

a

Du gehst dahin, um zu Hause anzurufen.

b

Verlorene Gegenstände können hier abgeholt werden.

c

Du kannst hier Tag und Nacht Geld abheben.

d

Hier kann man sich ein Fahrrad mieten.

Beispiel: a – das ist die Telefonzelle.

Q Two of the places listed are not described. Describe them yourself.

B On the telephone

WRITE

1 Wie sagt man das auf deutsch?
Write down the German for the following phrases.

a) Johann speaking.

b) Hello.

c) Goodbye.

d) Just a moment, please.

e) Who is speaking, please?

f) Could I leave a message, please?

g) Sorry, he is not here at the moment.

h) I'll ring again later.

Q Practise using the telephone for a conversation in German.

2 Schreibe einen Telefondialog.
Write a script for a telephone call.

C Changing money

SPEAK

Remember
To talk about money, just put the number with the currency (e.g. einhundert Euro, zwanzig Pfund, sechzig Schweizer Franken).

Q Race a friend to say or write them correctly when you turn over a piece of paper with numbers and currencies written on.

1 Sage die Nummer unten.
Say the numbers below.

a) **20**
b) **100**
c) **10**
d) **30**
e) *50*
f) **75**
g) *250*

2 Mache Dialoge.
Make up dialogues.

Beispiel:

✪ Ich möchte zwanzig Pfund tauschen.
✱ *In Schweizer Franken?*
✪ Nein, ich möchte Euros.
✱ *Ist das alles?*
✪ Ja, danke.

a	€20	→	SF
b	SF100	→	£
c	€125	→	£
d	£200	→	SF

PRACTICE

Im Fundbüro

1 Match the German phrases to the English.

What the official might say		
1	How can I help you?	a	Welche Farbe?
2	When did you lose it?	b	Wann haben Sie ihn/sie/es verloren?
3	Where did you lose it?	c	Wie kann ich Ihnen helfen?
4	What does it look like?	d	Wo haben Sie ihn/sie/es verloren?
5	What colour?	e	Wie sieht er/sie/es aus?

2 Now write what you might say.

a I've lost my watch.
b Three hours ago.
c Somewhere in the museum.
d It has a leather strap.
e Brown.

3 Put the conversation together and perform it.

Make sure you're familiar with all of the question words (wann, wie, wo, warum, welche, wer).

THE BARE
BONES

➤ Make sure you know all the parts of the body and how to describe what is the matter with them.

➤ Being able to describe where you are is also important in any emergency.

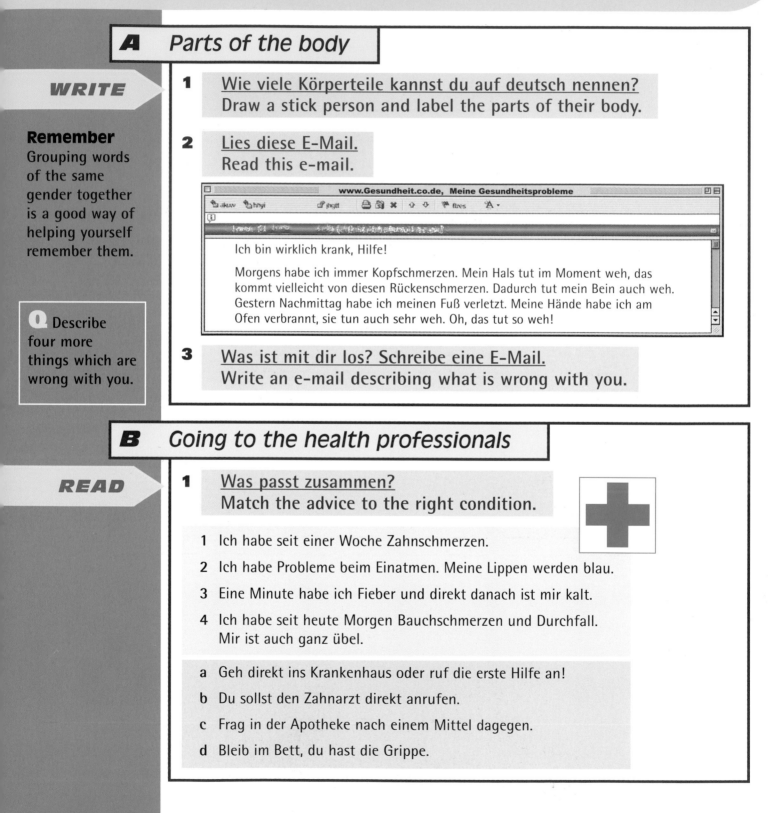

A Parts of the body

WRITE

1 Wie viele Körperteile kannst du auf deutsch nennen?
Draw a stick person and label the parts of their body.

Remember
Grouping words of the same gender together is a good way of helping yourself remember them.

2 Lies diese E-Mail.
Read this e-mail.

---

www.Gesundheit.co.de, Meine Gesundheitsprobleme

Ich bin wirklich krank, Hilfe!

Morgens habe ich immer Kopfschmerzen. Mein Hals tut im Moment weh, das kommt vielleicht von diesen Rückenschmerzen. Dadurch tut mein Bein auch weh. Gestern Nachmittag habe ich meinen Fuß verletzt. Meine Hände habe ich am Ofen verbrannt, sie tun auch sehr weh. Oh, das tut so weh!

Q Describe four more things which are wrong with you.

3 Was ist mit dir los? Schreibe eine E-Mail.
Write an e-mail describing what is wrong with you.

B Going to the health professionals

READ

1 Was passt zusammen?
Match the advice to the right condition.

1 Ich habe seit einer Woche Zahnschmerzen.

2 Ich habe Probleme beim Einatmen. Meine Lippen werden blau.

3 Eine Minute habe ich Fieber und direkt danach ist mir kalt.

4 Ich habe seit heute Morgen Bauchschmerzen und Durchfall.
Mir ist auch ganz übel.

a Geh direkt ins Krankenhaus oder ruf die erste Hilfe an!

b Du sollst den Zahnarzt direkt anrufen.

c Frag in der Apotheke nach einem Mittel dagegen.

d Bleib im Bett, du hast die Grippe.

C Emergency!

SPEAK

Remember
In Germany you should dial 110 in an emergency to get in touch with the police.

Q Underline any useful words and phrases in the conversations.

1 Lies diese Gespräche.
Read these conversations.

Guten Tag, Polizeiwache, Haben Sie ein Problem?

Ja, Guten Tag. Ich habe eine Panne. Ich bin auf der Autobahn E20 nördlich von Michelhafen. Mein Name ist Frühling, das ist F-R-Ü-H-L-I-N-G und das Auto ist ein brauner BMW.

Guten Tag. Ich habe einen Unfall gehabt. Wir sind beide verletzt, aber nicht sehr schwer. Meine Name ist Salamander – S-A-L-A-M-A-N-D-E-R – und wir stehen auf der Straße zwischen Jockgrim und Kandel.

Bleiben Sie bitte am Wagen, wir schicken jemanden zu Ihnen sobald wie möglich.

2 Mache Dialoge.
Make new dialogues.

Name	Astrid	Stetner
Panne/Unfall	Panne	Unfall
Standort	Straße zwischen Landau und Germersheim	Neben der Brücke, Neuer Weg, Bad Marienberg
Was für einen Wagen?	Mercedes	Ford

PRACTICE

1 Find a full-length picture or poster of a famous person. Label as many parts of their body as you can. Write a few sentences about what is wrong with each part.

Memorise and practise a few general phrases that can be used in a variety of situations. In your preparation time before the speaking exam, decide which phrases you are going to use. Then all you have to do is remember to include them!

Vocabulary

A Services

Ich möchte einen Brief nach Amerika schicken.	I would like to send a letter to America.
Was kostet es, eine Postkarte nach England zu schicken?	How much does it cost to send a postcard to England?
Gibt es eine Telefonzelle in der Nähe?	In there a phone box nearby?

Wie ist Ihre Telefonnummer?	What is your telephone number?
Kennen Sie die Vorwahlnummer?	Do you know the dialling code?
am Apparat	speaking
Ich möchte bitte mit Frau Braun sprechen.	I'd like to speak to Mrs Braun please.
Ist Karl da?	Is Karl there?
Wer spricht, bitte?	Who is it, please?
Einen Augenblick, bitte.	One moment, please.
Kann ich bitte eine Nachricht hinterlassen?	Can I leave a message, please?
Er/sie ist im Moment leider nicht da.	I'm sorry, he/she isn't here moment.
Ich versuche, Sie zu verbinden.	I'm trying to connect you.
Sagen Sie ihm, dass Maria angerufen hat.	Tell him that Maria phoned.
Kann er mich zurückrufen?	Can he call me back?

die Apotheke	chemist's	das Reisebüro	travel agent's
der Fahrradverleih	bike hire shop	der Reisescheck	traveller's cheque
das Fundbüro	lost property office	die Sparkasse	bank
der Geldautomat	cash machine	die Telefonzelle	phone booth
die Reinigung	dry cleaner's	die Wechselstube	bureau de change

B Health and safety

Wie geht's?	How are you?
Es geht./Es geht mir besser.	I'm alright, okay./I feel better.
Es geht mir nicht gut.	I don't feel well.
Was ist los?	What is the matter?
Mir ist kalt/heiß.	I feel cold/hot.
Ich habe Fieber.	I have a temperature.
Ich habe einen Schnupfen/Bauchschmerzen / Durchfall.	I've got a cold/stomach ache/ diarrhoea.
Wo tut es weh?	Where does it hurt?
Ich habe mir den Arm gebrochen.	I have broken my arm.
Mir ist auch ganz übel.	I also feel sick.
Guten Tag, Polizeiwache. Haben Sie ein Problem?	Hello, police station. Can I help you?
Ich habe eine Panne.	My car has broken down.
Ich habe einen Unfall gehabt.	I have had an accident.

B

der Erste-Hilfe-Kasten	*first aid box*	der Notruf	*emergency call*
die Feuerwehr	*fire brigade*	die Polizei	*police*
gefährlich	*dangerous*	verletzt	*wounded*
der Krankenwagen	*ambulance*		

Grammar

C Modal verbs

1 You use the verb **möchten** to talk about what you **would like** to do. Do you remember the rule for phrases like this?

> part of **möchte** + infinitive at the end
>
> Ich **möchte** die Türkei **entdecken**.
>
> Sie **möchte** in die Berge **fahren**.

Q Write about the things you would like to do next year, using möchten.

2 To talk about what you **must** do, use **müssen**. The rule is the same as for **möchten**.

> part of **müssen** + infinitive at the end
>
> Man **muss** lange **studieren**.
>
> Ich **muss** Abitur **machen**.

Q Write about the things you must do this week, using müssen.

3 It's the same rule with **können** (ich kann), **sollen** (ich soll), **dürfen** (ich darf) too!

Q Write about some things you can, should or are allowed to do.

D Future tense

1 Look at how the future tense is formed:

> right part of **werden** + infinitive at the end
>
> Ich **werde** in die Stadt **fahren**.
>
> Ich **werde** in die Disko **gehen**.

The infinitive goes to the end again – just like before with **müssen**, **möchten**, **dürfen**, **können** and **sollen**!

Q Talk about your plans for next week using the future tense.

If you need advice, contact the BITESIZE team on the Internet. The Web and e-mail addresses are on the back cover of this book.

Home life

THE BARE BONES

➤ Even if you only know a few verbs in the past tense, make sure you can use them correctly.

➤ Be sure you understand how **müssen** and separable verbs work and can use them correctly.

A Jobs around the house

WRITE

Remember
The verb <u>müssen</u> needs an infinitive at the end of the sentence.

1 <u>Lies diese Texte.</u>
Read these texts.

Jede Woche muss ich einkaufen gehen. Ich koche auch zweimal in der Woche. Das gefällt mir – ich kann was ich will für meine Mutter, meinen Vater und meine zwei Schwestern vorbereiten.

Udo

Ich helfe soviel wie möglich zu Hause. Ich decke den Tisch, leere die Mülltonne, mache mein Bett, trockne ab und füttere meinen Hund. Das ist ziemlich viel im Vergleich mit meinen Freunden.

Silke

Abends spüle ich ab. Ich muss auch mein Zimmer aufräumen und einmal in der Woche staubsaugen. Das finde ich nicht besonders schwierig. Am Wochenende putze ich auch öfters das Auto meines Vaters. Ich bekomme dafür zehn Mark!

Mehmet

2 Was müssen diese Leute tun? Schreibe es auf.
What do these people have to do? Write it down.

Marko
wash up and dry

Matthias
put out the rubbish once a week

Sylvia
keep her room tidy
make her bed

B Helping at home

SPEAK

Q Say some sentences describing any housework you did last week.

1 <u>Was haben sie gemacht?</u>
Describe what the six people in Part A did.
Use the past tense.

Beispiel:

Udo **ist** einkaufen **gegangen**.

Er **hat** das Essen **vorbereitet**.

Look at page 55 to help you.

C Meals

READ

1 Lies den Text.
Read the text.

Jeden Tag frühstücke ich mit der Familie. Es gibt Cornflakes oder Müsli, Orangensaft und Obst. Ich trinke auch sehr gern Tee mit Milch und Zucker – mindestens zwei Tassen. Mittags esse ich in der Schule. Das ist nicht besonders gut, ist aber billig und im Winter schön warm. Wenn wir Glück haben, gibt es Suppe oder Hähnchen mit Pommes, normalerweise aber müssen wir zwischen Pizza, Currywurst oder belegten Brötchen wählen. Abends esse ich wieder zusammen mit meiner Familie. Meine Mutter kocht jeden Abend etwas Gutes – vielleicht Spaghetti Bolognese, chinesisches Stir Fry oder sogar Steak. Das schmeckt immer sehr gut! Ich esse aber lieber Tomatensuppe mit Toast – das ist mein Lieblingsessen! Am Wochenende unternehme ich normalerweise etwas Tolles mit meinem Freund. Am Samstag haben wir ein richtiges Englisches Frühstück in einem Café gegessen – Spiegeleier, Toast, Speck, Bohnen in Tomatensoße und Würstchen.

2 Was isst sie? Schreibe eine Liste.
What does she eat? Write a list.

Remember
You may not be able to understand every word in a text, but keep reading and understand what you can.

Q What do you like to eat? Use **gern, lieber** and **am liebsten**.

PRACTICE

1 Write a letter to your pen pal. Describe:
- what you eat for breakfast, lunch and your evening meal
- what you like to eat
- how you help at home
- whether you like it
- if you get pocket money.

In the exam, check whether you have to write a letter (**der Brief**), a postcard (**die Postkarte**), a report (**der Bericht**), notes (**die Notizen**) or an advert (**der Werbetext**) and make sure to do what's asked. Practise all of these styles.

Healthy living

THE BARE BONES

➤ It is useful to be able to speak and write about a healthy lifestyle. Food and exercise are two important parts of this.

➤ Being able to make comparisons will help you to express an opinion, which, as you know, is very important at GCSE.

A Healthy eating

WRITE

1 Frau Schwer möchte abnehmen. Sie schreibt auf, was sie gestern gegessen hat.
Frau Schwer wants to lose weight. She has written down everything she ate yesterday.

Frühstück Cornflakes mit Milch und Zucker, Toast mit Butter und Marmelade x3, vier Scheiben Schinken mit Brötchen, Butter, Tasse Kaffee mit Milch und Zucker

Zweites Frühstück Brezel, eine Tasse Kaffee mit Milch und Zucker

Mittagessen Currywurst mit Pommes, Banane, ein Glas Orangensaft

Nachmittag Kaffee und Kuchen

Abendessen Thunfisch in Öl, Salat mit Tomaten, Käse, Würstchen, Kartoffeln, Schokoladeneis

Q Describe what Frau Schwer ate yesterday. Use the words **sehr gesund, ungesund, nicht besonders gesund** and **gefährlich!**

2 Schlage einen Diätplan vor, um Frau Schwer zu helfen.
Suggest a diet plan for Frau Schwer.

Obst Gemüse Fisch ohne Öl Salat	ist/wäre	besser als ... gesünder als ... am besten. am gesündesten.	Hamburger. Pommes. Schokolade.

B Sports and lifestyle

READ

1 Mache eine Liste von Sportverben auf deutsch.
List as many verbs for doing **sports** as you can think of in German.

Remember
There are lots of ways to learn vocabulary – write words down several times.

B

2 <u>Ich ...</u>
Write down the **ich** form of each verb.

Beispiel: ich segle, ich tanze ...

3 <u>Was hast du gemacht?</u>
Write a sentence in the past tense using each verb.

Use Grammar page 55 to help you.

Beispiel: Gestern bin ich gesegelt. Letzte Woche haben wir getanzt.

C Getting fit

READ

1 <u>Wer soll welches Poster lesen?</u>
Who should read which poster/s?

Remember
There may be more than one possible answer, so give all the possibilities which could be right!

Q Write an article about the last year for one of the people in Question C1. What did they do to achieve their goals? What will they do in the coming year?

(a)

Max: möchte eine Herausforderung

Friedrich: möchte abnehmen

Rin: möchte Fitness verbessern

Herballink

Abnehmen – ein Kilo pro Woche – ohne Zweifel – Garantiert!

Nichts Verbotenes! Essen Sie was Sie wollen!

Sie können wie vor zehn Jahren aussehen!

www.Herballink.de.com

(b)

SCHWIMMEN	LAUFEN	FAHRRAD FAHREN
2km	10km	20km

Triathlon Trier
16. März

letzte Bewerbung 16. Januar
Telefon: 05439 32 45 27

(c)

Fitness-Studio Frank

Komm dazu! Mach dich fit!

Es kostet nicht viel und kann das Leben verbessern!

Ruf 07770 25247 an

PRACTICE

1 Write about your diet and fitness. What were you like a year ago, what are you like today, what do you intend to do next year and why? Do you feel good?

In the exam, you don't have to tell the truth – use your language to impress – don't worry if it's not true!

A Home life

Remember
In the exam, you should always try to use present, past and future tenses and express an opinion.

abspülen	*to wash up*	das Geschirr	*the dishes*
abtrocknen	*to dry up*	der Haushalt	*household*
aufpassen	*to look after (children)*	kochen	*to cook*
aufräumen	*to tidy up*	leeren	*to empty*
bügeln	*to iron*	die Mülltonne	*rubbish bin*
decken	*to lay (the table)*	putzen	*to clean*
einkaufen	*to shop*	staubsaugen	*to hoover*
füttern	*to feed (an animal)*	vorbereiten	*to prepare*

ich mag ...	*I like ...*	ich finde ... nicht gut	*I don't like ...*
... gefällt mir		es gefällt mir nicht	
ich finde ... gut		ich mag das nicht	
Das ist toll.	*That's great.*	Das ist schrecklich.	*That's awful.*

B Healthy living

das Abendessen	*evening meal*	das Frühstück	*breakfast*
abnehmen	*to lose weight*	gefährlich	*dangerous*
die Ananas	*pineapple*	gesund	*healthy*
der Apfel	*apple*	die grünen Bohnen	*green beans*
der Appetit	*appetite*	das Mittagessen	*midday meal*
die Aprikose	*apricot*	das Steak	*steak*
die Banane	*banana*	ungesund	*unhealthy*
das Bier	*beer*	der Vegetarier	*vegetarian*
die Birne	*pear*	das Vitamin	*vitamin*
der Blumenkohl	*cauliflower*	zunehmen	*to put on weight*

Grammar

C Some irregular verbs

1 The verbs **haben** and **sein** are important for forming the past tense. They do not follow the same pattern as other verbs, so you need to learn them.

	haben	sein
ich	habe	bin
du	hast	bist
er/sie/es/man	hat	ist
wir	haben	sind
ihr	habt	seid
Sie/sie	haben	sind

 Make up ten sentences using the verbs **haben** and **sein**.

D The dative case

The dative case is often used when the word **to** comes in front of a noun in English. All the words for **a** and **the** change in the dative.

Masculine	Ich sage das **dem** Arzt.	I'll tell that to the doctor.
	Ich gebe es **einem** Freund.	I'll give it to a friend.
Feminine	Ich schicke **der** Lehrerin den Brief.	I'll send the letter to the teacher.
	Ich gebe **einer** Lehrerin das Geld.	I'll give the money to a teacher.
Neuter	Ich bringe es **dem** Mädchen.	I'll take it to the girl.
	Er gibt **einem** Kind das Geschenk.	He gives the present to a child.

Remember
my, your, etc. change in the same way as ein, eine and ein.

E Prepositions

1 Prepositions are words which tell you where something is. The following prepositions must always be followed by the **accusative** case.

für *for*	bis *until*	ohne *without*	durch *through*

Ich arbeite für **meinen** Vater.
Ich gehe ohne **meine** Familie.
Ich komme ohne **mein** Kind.

2 a The following prepositions are always followed by the **dative** in German.

aus	out of	nach	after
bei	at the home of	seit	since
gegenüber	opposite	von	from
mit	with, by	zu	to

Er kommt **aus dem** Haus.
Er sitzt **gegenüber dem** Rathaus.
Wir arbeiten **nach der** Schule.

b **zu dem** is often shortened to **zum**, and **zu der** to **zur**.

Wie komme ich **zum** Schloss?
Ich fahre mit dem Bus **zur** Schule.

3 For prepositions that can be followed by the **dative** or the **accusative**, see page 67.

Remember
When you are able to use words given to help you, make 100% sure that you don't make unnecessary mistakes copying.

Q Using the prepositions above, describe where things are in your house.

Jobs and work experience

THE BARE BONES

➤ You may be asked to write or speak about jobs and money, or to write a letter applying for a job.

➤ Make sure you can understand and use **some** verbs in the future.

A Part-time work or pocket money?

WRITE

1 <u>Lies den Text.</u>
Read the text.

> Samstags und manchmal
> in der Woche arbeite ich bei meinem Onkel
> in seinem Lebensmittelgeschäft. Die Arbeit ist interessant
> und ich habe die Gelegenheit verschiedene Leute kennenzulernen.
> Es gefällt mir sehr. Ich bekomme €10 pro Stunde. Ich gebe
> mein Geld für Kleider, CDs, Zeitschriften und Süßigkeiten aus.
> Seitdem ich einen Job habe, bekomme ich kein
> Taschengeld mehr. Wenn ich älter bin, möchte ich in
> einem Geschäft arbeiten.

Remember
To make jobs feminine, all you need to do is add **–in** at the end! (Sometimes there is also an umlaut, like Ärztin, Köchin.)

2 <u>Schreibe einen ähnlichen Text für diese Schülerin.</u>
Write a similar text for this student.

- Michaela

- likes the work; enjoys meeting people

- works in a clothes shop

- no pocket money

- gets €12 an hour and works six hours on a Saturday

- spends her money on clothes and magazines from the shop

- would like to be a translator when she is older

Q Do you have a part-time job? Do you get pocket money?

B Professions and career

SPEAK

1 <u>Ordne die Wörter um Berufe zu finden.</u>
Unjumble the words to find the jobs.

Q Add other professions to your list.

a **OchK**

b **Mhcenikera**

c **trgerBräief**

d genurIine

e **Pozlisti**

f lleKnre

C Job application

WRITE

1 Lies diesen Brief.
Read this letter.

London, den 17. Januar

Sehr geehrte Frau Schilling!

Ich heiße Elizabeth Townend und ich bin 16 Jahre alt. Mein Lehrer hat mir Ihre Anzeige für ein Au Pair Mädchen/Junge gezeigt.

Ich habe eine Schwester und einen Bruder. Ich habe immer Babysitting für meine Eltern gemacht, und weil meine Mutter arbeitet, bin ich daran gewöhnt mich um die Kinder zu kümmern. Es gefällt mir auch sehr, Zeit mit kleinen Kindern zu verbringen.

Ich lerne seit fünf Jahren Deutsch und möchte sehr gern mein Deutsch verbessern. Zwei Monate in Deutschland werden mir sicherlich dabei helfen. Ich könnte am 1. Juli anfangen.

Ich schicke mit diesem Brief meinen Lebenslauf und freue mich auf Ihre Antwort.

Mit freundlichem Gruß,

Ihre
Elizabeth Townend

2 Schreibe eine Stellenbewerbung. Mache zuerst einen Plan.
Write a job application. Make a plan first.

PRACTICE

1 Imagine you are in a job interview. Answer these questions, adding any extra information you can.

- Wie heißt du?
- Wie alt bist du?
- Wo wohnst du?
- Wie ist deine Adresse?
- Wie ist deine Telefonnummer?
- In was für eine Schule gehst du?
- In welcher Klasse bist du?
- Was sind deine Lieblingsfächer?
- Was für Hobbys hast du?
- Was möchtest du später werden?

To help with speaking activities, record yourself asking the questions. Then record yourself giving answers, perhaps even with a camcorder.

THE BARE
BONES

➤ In the exam, you might be asked to use the telephone, a letter or another method to organise going out.

➤ When organising going out, you'll need the future tense.

A Things to do in your spare time

READ

1 <u>Verbinde die richtige Person mit dem passenden Poster.</u>
Match the right poster with the right person.

Q Which poster appeals to you most? Why?

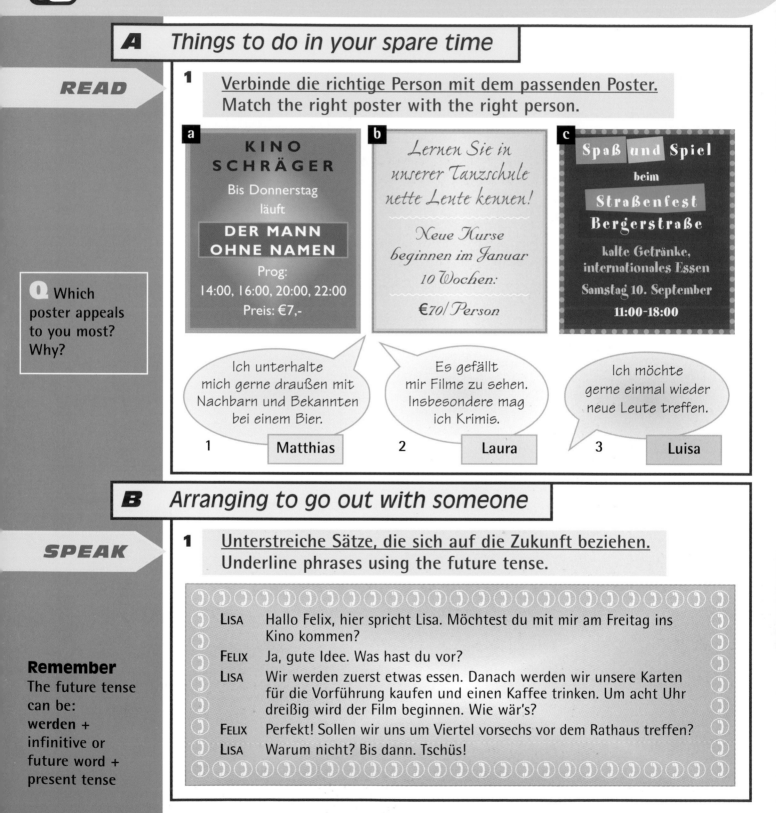

a
KINO SCHRÄGER
Bis Donnerstag läuft
DER MANN OHNE NAMEN
Prog:
14:00, 16:00, 20:00, 22:00
Preis: €7,-

b
Lernen Sie in unserer Tanzschule nette Leute kennen!
Neue Kurse beginnen im Januar 10 Wochen:
€70/Person

c
Spaß und Spiel
beim
Straßenfest
Bergerstraße
kalte Getränke, internationales Essen
Samstag 10. September
11:00-18:00

Ich unterhalte mich gerne draußen mit Nachbarn und Bekannten bei einem Bier.

Es gefällt mir Filme zu sehen. Insbesondere mag ich Krimis.

Ich möchte gerne einmal wieder neue Leute treffen.

1 Matthias | 2 Laura | 3 Luisa

B Arranging to go out with someone

SPEAK

1 <u>Unterstreiche Sätze, die sich auf die Zukunft beziehen.</u>
Underline phrases using the future tense.

LISA   Hallo Felix, hier spricht Lisa. Möchtest du mit mir am Freitag ins Kino kommen?

FELIX   Ja, gute Idee. Was hast du vor?

LISA   Wir werden zuerst etwas essen. Danach werden wir unsere Karten für die Vorführung kaufen und einen Kaffee trinken. Um acht Uhr dreißig wird der Film beginnen. Wie wär's?

FELIX   Perfekt! Sollen wir uns um Viertel vorsechs vor dem Rathaus treffen?

LISA   Warum nicht? Bis dann. Tschüs!

Remember
The future tense can be:
werden +
infinitive or
future word +
present tense

B **2** <u>Mache einen Dialog.</u>
Create a conversation.

C *Planning a trip*

WRITE

1 <u>Lies diesen Brief.</u>
Read this letter.

> Frankfurt, den 19. März
>
> **Lieber Jon!**
>
> **Ich freue mich sehr auf deinen Besuch. Hier gibt es für junge Leute so viel zu tun! Wir könnten ins Kino gehen. Wir werden vielleicht ein Abend in die Stadt fahren und einen neuen Film anschauen! Oder vielleicht möchtest du lieber einen Stadtbummel machen. Wir werden uns im Café entspannen und übers Leben reden.**
>
> **Schreibe mir bald und sag, was dich interessiert!**
>
> **Dein Lukas**

2 <u>Schreibe einen Brief an Lukas.</u>
Write an answer to Lukas.

- Say what you like to do.
- Say what you think about his suggestions.
- Give reasons for your opinions.
- Add a suggestion of your own.
- Say that you are also looking forward to the visit.

PRACTICE

1 You are on a German exchange. Write an e-mail saying what you have done this week and what you will do next week.

THIS WEEK	NEXT WEEK
went skating	theatre – not sure what we'll be seeing!
went swimming	go shopping in the town centre
went to Cologne (Köln) by train for the day	climb to the top of the cathedral
went to the cinema to see Shrek – brilliant!	

The letter in Part C is about 70 words long. Practice writing letters of this length.

Vocabulary

A Part-time jobs and work experience

Was macht dein Bruder?	What does your brother do?
Er ist arbeitslos.	He's unemployed.
Er arbeitet in einem Büro.	He works in an office.
Ich trage Zeitungen aus.	I deliver newspapers.
Samstags arbeite ich als Kellner.	I work as a waiter on Saturdays.
Hast du ein Arbeitspraktikum gemacht?	Have you done work experience?
Ja, ich habe zwei Wochen in einem Geschäft gearbeitet.	Yes, I worked for two weeks in a shop.
Arbeitest du am Wochenende?	Do you work at the weekends?
Ich arbeite als Babysitter.	I work as a babysitter.
Ich bekomme drei Pfund pro Stunde.	I get three pounds an hour.
Es ist langweilig, aber ich brauche das Geld.	It's boring but I need the money.
Mein Vater ist Verkäufer.	My father is a salesman.
Meine Mutter ist Ärztin.	My mother is a doctor.
Ich möchte Krankenschwester werden.	I'd like to become a nurse.

die Arbeit	work	der Koch/die Köchin	cook
das Arbeitspraktikum	work experience	der Lehrer/	teacher
der Arzt/die Ärztin	doctor	die Lehrerin	
der Beruf	job/profession	der Lehrgang	training
der Briefträger/	postman/	der Lohn	salary
die Briefträgerin	postwoman	der Mechaniker/	mechanic
das Büro	office	die Mechanikerin	
die Fabrik	factory	der Polizist/	policeman/
die Firma	company	die Polizistin	policewoman
der Ingenieur/	engineer	sparen	to save (money)
die Ingenieurin		die Stelle	position/job
der Kellner/	waiter/waitress	der Teilzeitjob	part-time job
die Kellnerin		verdienen	to earn

B Leisure

Fasching	Carnival (celebrated in February)	die Eisdiele	ice cream parlour
		der Flohmarkt	fleamarket
der Heiligabend	Christmas Eve	die Freizeitbe-	pastime
der Karneval	carnival	schäftigung	
das Neujahr	New Year's Day	kennenlernen	to get to know
das Ostern	Easter	das Straßenfest	street festival
Silvester	New Year's Eve	die Tanzschule	dancing school
Weihnachten	Christmas	das Theaterstück	play
der erste Januar	1 January	treffen	to meet
der fünfundzwanzigste Dezember	25 December	die Vorführung	showing (film)
		weltberühmt	world famous
beschäftigt	busy	zufrieden	satisfied
einkaufen	to shop		

C The perfect tense

1 Many regular verbs take **haben** in the perfect tense.

part of **haben** + past participle (**ge...t** or **ge...en**) at the end

Ich **habe** Tennis **gespielt**. (from **spielen**)
Er **hat** einen Keks **gegessen**. (from **essen**)

2 Separable verbs take **haben** and the **ge** comes in the middle. For example:

Wir **haben** nach dem Essen ab**ge**spült und ab**ge**trocknet.
Sie **hat** ihr Zimmer auf**ge**räumt.

3 There are some irregular verbs which take **haben**. The past participle doesn't have a **ge**. For example:

Ich **habe** €10 **bekommen**.
Er **hat** das Abendessen **vorbereitet**.

4 Verbs of movement take **sein**.

part of **sein** + past participle (**ge...en**) at the end

Ich **bin** in die Stadt **gegangen**. (from **gehen**)
Sie **ist** zu ihrem Freund **gefahren**. (from **fahren**)

See page 61 for more on this.

Q Say five things you did yesterday using the perfect tense.

D Possessives

The words for **my**, **your**, **her**, **his**, **our** and **their** have the same endings as the word **ein**.

Meine Schwester wohnt bei **meiner** Mutter.	My sister lives with my mother.
Deine Freundin hat **ihre** Tasche dabei.	Your girlfriend has her bag with her.
Sein Auto steht vor **seinem** Haus.	His car is in front of his house.
Unser Hund ist in **unserem** Haus.	Our dog is in our house.
Ihr Kind ist in **seinem** Bett.	Their child is in his bed.

2 In German, you can show who owns something by adding an **s** to names, like in English but without the apostrophe.

Das ist **Sandras** Bruder.   That is Sandra's brother.

Q Make up sentences using possessives.

Don't panic when you first turn over your exam paper. Just work your way through the activities one by one.

At the shops

THE BARE BONES

➤ You will need to use and/or recognise the language used to buy various items.

➤ Make sure you know the polite language to use when talking to a shopkeeper.

➤ Don't be put off by words on signs or posters that you don't understand – you may not need to understand them for the task.

A Shopping list

WRITE

1 <u>Schreibe eine Einkaufsliste.</u>
Write a shopping list.

| 1 _____ | 2 _____ | 3 _____ | 4 _____ |
| 5 _____ | 6 _____ | 7 _____ | 8 _____ |

Remember
Make sure you give the number of items requested in a list – no more, and no less.

B Choosing which food to buy

READ

1 <u>Was kann man nicht essen?</u>
Which items aren't edible?

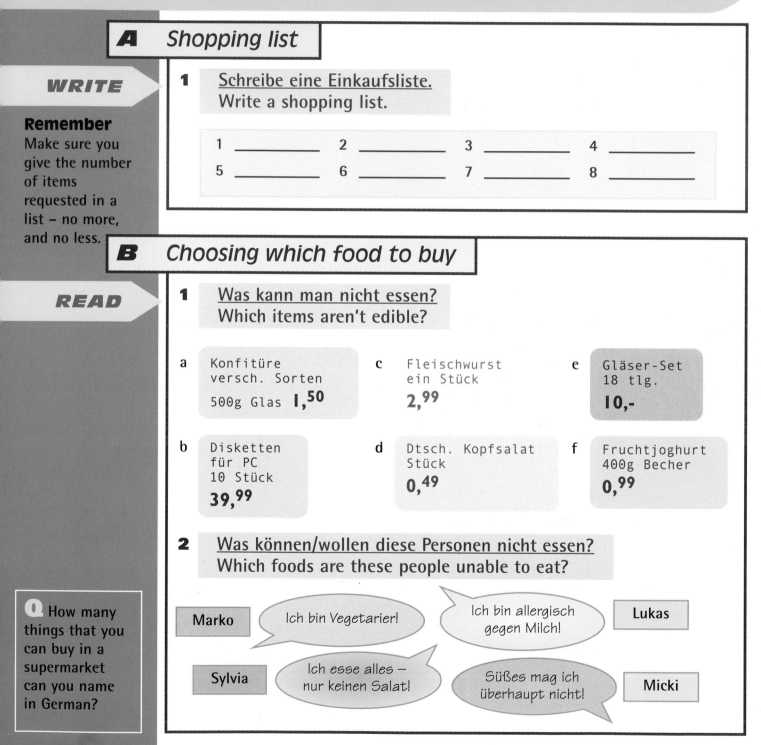

a Konfitüre
versch. Sorten
500g Glas **1,50**

c Fleischwurst
ein Stück
2,99

e Gläser-Set
18 tlg.
10,-

b Disketten
für PC
10 Stück
39,99

d Dtsch. Kopfsalat
Stück
0,49

f Fruchtjoghurt
400g Becher
0,99

2 <u>Was können/wollen diese Personen nicht essen?</u>
Which foods are these people unable to eat?

Marko — Ich bin Vegetarier!

Ich bin allergisch gegen Milch! — Lukas

Sylvia — Ich esse alles – nur keinen Salat!

Süßes mag ich überhaupt nicht! — Micki

Q How many things that you can buy in a supermarket can you name in German?

C At the counter

SPEAK

1 Sage diese Wörter auf deutsch.
Say these items in German.

a 1 bottle of lemonade   c piece of cheese   e 6 bread rolls

b 200g ham   d bar of chocolate   f tin of carrots

2 Mache einen Dialog.
Make up a shopping dialogue.

Beispiel:

★ *Ja bitte?*

☆ Ich hätte gern ein Kilo Orangen.

★ *Bitte. Sonst noch etwas?*

☆ Ich möchte drei Würstchen.

★ *Hier. Ist das alles?*

☆ Und ein Paket Kekse, bitte.

★ *Bitte sehr.*

☆ Vielen Dank.

Q Put the food words into sentences:
Ich hätte gerne ...
Ich habe ... gekauft.
Wo finde ich ...?

Remember
You will only need to learn the customer's part – the examiner will play the shopkeeper.

PRACTICE

1 Look at these shop signs. Underline the words you don't understand.

1 **ELEKTRO-FISCHER Für alles Elektronische!**

2 *Die Vollkornbäckerei Brenner* Alle Sorten Brot, Brötchen, Kuchen und, und, und!

3 **Hohner Musikinstrumente** Gitarren sind unsere Spezialität

2 Where can you buy these items?

a Brötchen

b ein PC

c eine Gitarre

You will often not understand every word of a written activity. Don't let this worry you. Look at how many words you did not need to do this activity successfully!

At the department store

➤ Being able to find your way around a building is useful when you are shopping and in other situations.

➤ Saying what is the matter and dealing with problems are important skills.

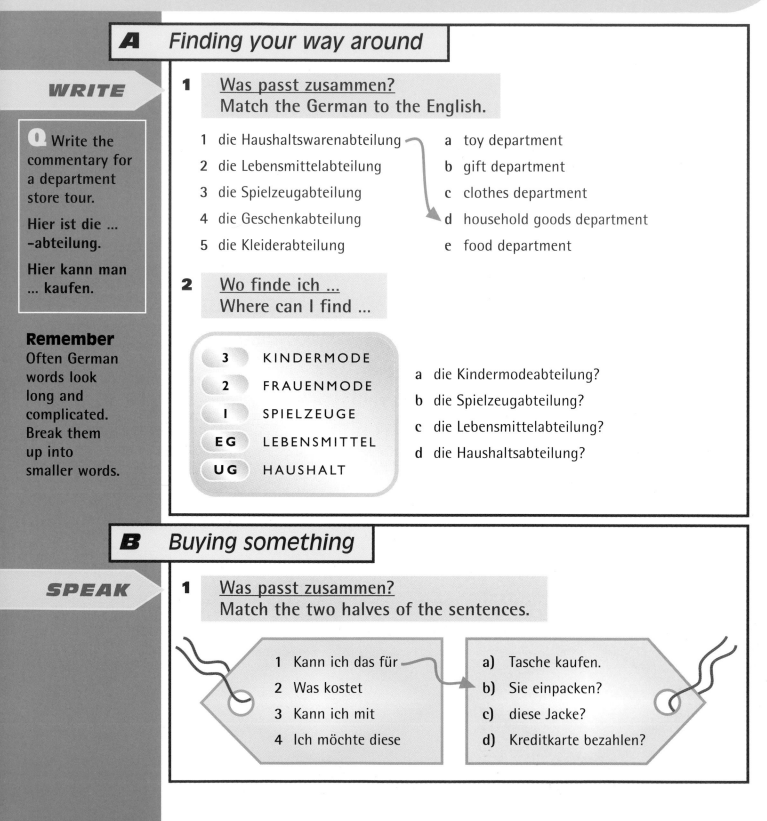

A Finding your way around

WRITE

Q Write the commentary for a department store tour.

Hier ist die ... -abteilung.

Hier kann man ... kaufen.

Remember
Often German words look long and complicated. Break them up into smaller words.

1 <u>Was passt zusammen?</u>
Match the German to the English.

1 die Haushaltswarenabteilung   a toy department

2 die Lebensmittelabteilung   b gift department

3 die Spielzeugabteilung   c clothes department

4 die Geschenkabteilung   d household goods department

5 die Kleiderabteilung   e food department

2 <u>Wo finde ich ...</u>
Where can I find ...

3	KINDERMODE
2	FRAUENMODE
1	SPIELZEUGE
E G	LEBENSMITTEL
U G	HAUSHALT

a die Kindermodeabteilung?

b die Spielzeugabteilung?

c die Lebensmittelabteilung?

d die Haushaltsabteilung?

B Buying something

SPEAK

1 <u>Was passt zusammen?</u>
Match the two halves of the sentences.

1 Kann ich das für   a) Tasche kaufen.

2 Was kostet   b) Sie einpacken?

3 Kann ich mit   c) diese Jacke?

4 Ich möchte diese   d) Kreditkarte bezahlen?

C Putting things right

READ

1 <u>Welche Antwort passt zu welchem Problem?</u>
Match the problems and the responses.

1
Ich habe diese Gläser gekauft. Als ich sie aus der Tüte herausgenommen habe, wusste ich, dass sie zu groß sind. Ich habe die Quittung hier. Kann ich sie bitte umtauschen?

a)
Ja, die Farbe steht Ihnen wirklich nicht besonders gut. Was hätten Sie denn gerne an Stelle der Bluse?

2
Meine Mutter hat mir diese Bluse gekauft. Die Farbe ist wirklich nichts für mich. Ich möchte lieber etwas anders zu meinem Geburtstag haben!

b)
Sie haben recht, die Wurst ist wirklich nicht in Ordnung. Möchten Sie eine andere Wurst oder lieber Ihr Geld zurück?

3
Heute Morgen erst habe ich diese Wurst gekauft, finde aber, dass sie sehr merkwürdig riecht. Meiner Meinung nach ist sie schlecht.

c)
Mit Kassenbon ist es gar kein Problem, die Gläser umzutauschen. Hier, suchen Sie sich bitte eine andere Größe aus.

2 <u>Lies das Gespräch und mache Dialoge.</u>
Read the conversation and make up dialogues.

★ *Guten Tag, kann ich Ihnen helfen?*

☆ Ja, Ich möchte ein Hemd kaufen.

★ *Welche Farbe möchten Sie?*

☆ Weiß.

★ *Welche Größe?*

☆ 44.

★ *Hier habe ich drei Hemden.*

☆ Dieses nehme ich. Kann ich mit Kreditkarte bezahlen?

★ *Sicherlich.*

☆ Danke schön, auf Wiedersehen.

| blue dress (size 36) | 4 large tea cups | a pair of jeans |

Remember
In the exam you will be recorded. Record yourself during your revision time to get used to this.

PRACTICE

1 What can you buy in each of these shops?

＋
Apotheke Schmidt

Santa Schmuck

Metzgerei Schanke

Learn different ways to say what you think of something.

Vocabulary

A At the shops

Gibt es hier eine Apotheke in der Nähe?	*Is there a chemist nearby?*
Wo gibt es einen Supermarkt?	*Where is there a supermarket?*
Wo ist die nächste Bäckerei?	*Where is the nearest baker's?*
Wo kann ich Apfelsaft kaufen?	*Where can I buy apple juice?*
Verkaufen Sie Cornflakes?	*Do you sell cornflakes?*
Wann macht die Metzgerei auf?	*When does the butcher's open?*
Wann schließt die Bank?	*When does the bank close?*
Sie ist bis vierzehn Uhr geschlossen.	*It is closed until 2pm.*

alles	*everything*	der Markt	*market*
die Apotheke	*chemist*	die Metzgerei	*butcher's*
die Brieftasche	*wallet*	offen	*open*
das Einkaufszentrum	*shopping centre*	öffnen	*to open*
das Geld	*money*	die Öffnungszeit	*opening time*
die Geschäftszeit	*business hours*	das Paket	*parcel*
das Geschenk	*present*	das Portemonnaie	*purse*
geschlossen	*closed*	schließen	*to close*
kaufen	*to buy*	die Schachtel	*box*
das Kaufhaus	*department store*	der Schmuck	*jewellery*
kostenlos	*free of charge*	das Sonderangebot	*special offer*
die Konditorei	*cake shop*	der Supermarkt	*supermarket*
der Kunde/die Kundin	*customer*	die Tüte	*carrier bag*
der Laden	*shop*		
das Lebensmittel- geschäft	*food shop/grocer's*		

B At the department store

Ich möchte ...	*I would like ...*
Ich hätte gern(e)...	*I would like ...*
Wo finde ich Schreibwaren?	*Where will I find the stationery?*
Wo sind die Toiletten?	*Where are the toilets?*
Gibt es hier einen Parkplatz?	*Is there a car park here?*

die Abteilung	*department*	der Aufzug	*lift*
die Geschenkabteilung	*gift department*	die Größe	*size*
die Kleiderabteilung	*clothing department*	der Handschuh	*glove*
die Lebensmittelabteilung	*food department*	das Hemd	*shirt*
die Handarbeitsabteilung	*craft department*	die Hose	*trousers*
die Haushaltsabteilung	*household department*	die Jacke	*jacket*
die Spielzeugabteilung	*toy department*	das Kleid	*dress*
die Süßwarenabteilung	*confectionery department*	die Kleidung	*clothes*
		die Kreditkarte	*credit card*
anprobieren	*to try on (clothes)*	der Regenschirm	*umbrella*

 Ask a shop assistant where you will find everything on your shopping list.

Grammar

C *Haben* or *sein* in the perfect tense?

Q Which of these verbs take haben and which take sein?

wohnen, reisen, machen, fahren.

1 Verbs which use **sein** instead of **haben** in the perfect tense are usually 'action' or 'travel' verbs, which describe movement or change, such as **to go**, **to come**, **to fly**.

Wir **sind** in die Stadt gegangen.
Er **ist** nach Spanien geflogen.

D Comparatives

1 When you want to make a comparison between two things, take the adjective you want to use and, as a rule, add **-er**.

2 This applies to most adjectives, whatever their length.

Mathematik ist **leichter** als Englisch.
Maths is easier than English.

Kunst ist **interessanter** als Erdkunde.
Art is more interesting than geography.

3 Shorter adjectives like **groß** or **alt** add an umlaut on the vowels **a**, **o** and **u**.

Er ist **größer** und **älter als** ich.
He is taller and older than I am.

E Superlatives

Q Compare some of the people in your class. Write at least one sentence for each class member.

Superlatives are the most extreme forms of comparatives. That means they describe the best, the fastest or the most expensive. You add **-st** or **-est** to the adjective, and then the normal adjective ending.

Das ist mein **intelligentester Schüler**. This is my most intelligent student.
Er hat das **schnellste** Auto. He has the fastest car.

Make yourself a revision folder containing useful information. Carry it around with you and revise whenever you get time.

Character and relationships

THE BARE BONES

> ➤ It is important to be able to describe people's characteristics. It can help you to give fuller answers to questions in the exam.
> ➤ It is more important to get the general overall meaning of a text than to understand every word.

A Personality and character differences

WRITE

1 <u>Welche Wörter beschreiben dich, deine Eltern, deinen Freund/deine Freundin, deinen Lehrer / deine Lehrerin?</u>
Describe you, your parents, your friend, your teacher using these words.

Remember
Use a dictionary to check any words you don't know.

Q Compare the people (e.g. Meine Eltern sind optimistischer als mein Lehrer).

klug   humorlos   dumm   humorvoll   nett

streng   intelligent   lustig   modisch   altmodisch

faul   fleißig   hilfsbereit   optimistisch   launisch

geduldig   gestresst   anspruchsvoll   liebevoll   lieb

freundlich   witzig   praktisch   kompliziert   doof

langweilig   diktatorisch   lebendig   schüchtern

B Characteristics of a good friend

SPEAK

1 <u>Beschreibe jede Person und entscheide ob sie gute Freunde sind.</u>
Describe each person and decide if they are a good friend.

Remember
When you are preparing for a task like this, write down words to help you.

Beispiel:

- *Wie findest du Monika?*

- Sie ist sehr nett, immer freundlich und hilfsbereit.

- *Ja, das finde ich auch! Monika ist eine gute Freundin!*

Lucia	Max
interesting, lively, funny, can be a bit bossy	intelligent, hardworking, optimistic, sometimes moody

C Personal problems

READ

1 **Verbinde den richtigen Ratschlag mit dem richtigen Brief.**
Match the right advice with the correct letter.

1 *Liebe Tante Maria!*

Mein Freund hat mir heute gesagt, dass er mich nicht mehr liebt. Er sagt, wir können immer noch Freunde sein. Ich werde ihn nie vergessen. Ich liebe ihn so und weiß nicht, was ich tun soll. Ohne ihn werde ich so traurig sein!

Katja, Aachen

2 *Liebe Tante Maria!*

Die Schule ist für mich im Moment so schwierig, dass ich zweifle, ob ich dieses Jahr überstehen werde. Ich bin in der zehnten Klasse. Ich lerne jeden Abend zu Hause und schreibe trotzdem eine schlechte Note nach der anderen.

Max, Dortmund

a Warum sprichst du nicht mit einem Lehrer?

b Du wirst diesen jungen Mann vergessen.

c Du könntest die Probleme mit einer Gruppe Freundinnen besprechen.

d Mindestens die Hälfte aus deiner Klasse wird sich genauso wie du fühlen.

Q Underline any words you don't understand. Find their meaning, gender and plural. Learn them!

PRACTICE

1 Choose a famous person. Describe:

- their physical appearance
- their character (you can make this up)
- who their friends are
- whether you think they are a good friend.
- why you think this.

Expressing an opinion makes your answers in the writing and speaking exams more interesting! Do it as often as you can – it will improve your grade!

THE BARE BONES

➤ Make sure you use verbs correctly. The **ich** form ends in **–e**, **du** ends in **–st**, etc. Always check them when you do any writing.

➤ Make sure you know a range of vocabulary and phrases relevant to the environment.

A Environmentally friendly or not?

READ

1 <u>Umweltfreundlich ✔ oder umweltfeindlich? ✖</u>
Are these things environmentally friendly or not?

a Die Lichter in der Schule brennen den ganzen Tag. ✖

b Wenn möglich kauft meine Mutter Altpapier für zu Hause. ✔

c Wir haben zu Hause drei Mülleimer. Wir sortieren unseren Müll, so dass er recycelt werden kann.

d Ich weiß nicht, wo man Glas und Papier recyceln kann. Ich werfe es einfach weg.

e Ich kaufe mein Obst und Gemüse wenn möglich ohne Verpackung. Wir bringen von zu Hause Einkaufstaschen mit.

f Wir kompostieren unsere organischen Abfälle.

Remember
Many German words are similar to English (e.g. sortieren). Some words are made up of other words (e.g. Altpapier).

Q How environmentally friendly are you? Make up some sentences.

B Protecting the environment

SPEAK

1 <u>Bilde aus den Stichwörtern Sätze.</u>
Make sentences from the key words.

See page 43 for more information on **sollen** (should) and **müssen** (must).

Beispiel:

a Man **soll** nie Spraydosen **kaufen**, man **muss** immer Pumpspraydosen **kaufen**.

Nein	Ja
a) Spraydosen kaufen	Pumpspraydosen kaufen
b) mit dem Auto fahren	Fahrrad fahren/zu Fuß gehen
c) normales Reinigungsmittel kaufen	phosphatfreies Reinigungsmittel kaufen
d) Glasflaschen wegwerfen	Flaschen recyceln
e) Papier in den Mülleimer werfen	Papier in die grüne Tonne werfen
f) Jede Woche eine neue Plastiktüte nehmen	Taschen aus Stoff oder Altpapier benutzen

Remember
Spend time revising German rubrics. This really will help you in the exam!

C *Working together for the Earth*

WRITE

1   Lies den Brief.
Read the letter.

Bamberg, den 24. August

Liebe Natasha!

Diese Woche haben wir in der Schule Umweltwoche.

In Erdkunde lernen wir über die Regenwälder. Der Verlust an Bäumen trägt dazu bei, den Treibhauseffekt zu verschlechtern.

In Kunst lernen wir, wie man Altpapier machen kann. In der Schule recyclet man alle Papier.

In Naturwissenschaften haben wir Bäume gepflanzt. Ich habe eine Eiche vor der Schule selbst gepflanzt.

Zusätzlich ist diese Woche eine autofreie Woche. Das heißt, wir müssen alle mit dem Fahrrad, zu Fuß, mit dem Bus oder mit dem Zug kommen. Das hilft die Verschmutzung durch Autoemissionen zu vermindern.

Machst du etwas für die Umwelt? Erzähl ein bisschen darüber!

Deine Lisa

Remember
Using little words like nie (never), manchmal (sometimes) and immer (always) gives you the chance to show off!

2   Verarbeite die folgenden Informationen in einem Brief.
Write a letter including the following information.

- You went on an environment seminar last month.
- Describe what you did in the seminar.
- Describe what you learned about the environment.
- Describe what you do already to help the environment or what you're going to do from now on.

PRACTICE

1 Design a poster about protecting the environment. Here's a mini example! Write at least 100 words and make sure yours has much more information.

Flaschen nicht mehr wegwerfen!

Recyclen Sie alles mögliche!

For the speaking exam, it is worth preparing a few phrases for each topic. This will help in your written exam too!

Vocabulary

A Character and personal relationships

ein bisschen	a little/a bit	selten	rarely
ganz	quite	sehr	very
im allgemeinen	in general	total	totally
manchmal	sometimes	überhaupt nicht	not at all
nicht besonders	not especially	wirklich	really
nicht mehr	no more	ziemlich	quite
oft	often	zu	too

altmodisch	old-fashioned	kompliziert	complicated
anspruchsvoll	demanding	langweilig	boring
doof	silly	launisch	moody
dumm	stupid	lebendig	lively
faul	lazy	lieb	sweet
fleißig	hard-working	liebevoll	loving
freundlich	friendly	lustig	funny
geduldig	patient	modisch	fashionable
hilfsbereit	helpful	nett	nice
humorlos	humourless	schüchtern	shy
humorvoll	humorous	streng	strict
klug	bright	witzig	funny

B The environment

umweltfreundlich	environmentally friendly	umweltfeindlich	environmentally unfriendly

Wir sortieren unseren Müll, so dass er recycelt werden kann.	We sort our rubbish so that it can be recycled.
Ich fahre immer mit dem Rad.	I always travel by bike.
Ich kaufe mein Obst und Gemüse wenn möglich ohne Verpackung.	Whenever possible I buy my fruit and vegetables without packaging.
Wir bringen von zu Hause Einkaufstaschen mit.	We bring shopping bags with us from home.
Wir kompostieren unsere organischen Abfälle.	We compost our organic waste.
Ich kaufe immer Pfandflaschen.	I always buy returnable bottles.
Sonst versuche ich Glas oder Plastik mit dem grünen Punkt zu kaufen.	Otherwise, I try to buy glass or plastic which can be recycled.

der Abfall	rubbish	rauchen	to smoke
die Fußgängerzone	pedestrian zone	das Recycling	recycling
das Gebäude	building	die Umwelt	environment
die Hauptverkehrszeit	rush hour	die Umweltver-	pollution
der Lärm	noise	schmutzung	
die Luft	air	der Verkehrsstau	traffic jam
öffentlich	public	wegwerfen	to throw away

Grammar

Grammar

C Commands

1 Commands tell us what to do. In your German lessons, you probably hear your teacher use commands all the time. Look at the two commands below.

Macht die Tür zu!   **Hört** gut zu!

For this form of command, you just put the verb at the start of the sentence. These commands are for a group of people (**ihr**).

2 If commands are given to one pupil (**du**) they look slightly different:

Beantworte die Fragen!   **Ordne** die Sätze!

You may see commands like this in exam instructions.

3 There are also some exceptions, which look different again, but do the same job:

Lies den Text!   **Hör** zu!

4 When the commands are used in the polite form, then the **Sie** is used too:

Unterstreichen Sie …   **Stellen Sie** Fragen über …

5 If you put **nicht** after the verb, it becomes a negative instruction:

Vergessen Sie **nicht!**   **Don't** forget!

Q Write these commands in the correct order.

Fragen beantwortet die

Umfrage eine macht

Dialoge neue erfindet

D Sneaky prepositions

1 Some prepositions can be followed by either the **dative or** the **accusative** in German. The rule is:

- Use the accusative if the preposition is talking about **movement** towards a place.
- Use the dative if there is **no movement** implied by the preposition.

	ACCUSATIVE (movement)	DATIVE (no movement)
auf – on	Er setzt sich **auf das** Sofa. He sits down on the sofa.	Der Pulli ist **auf dem** Sofa. The jumper is on the sofa.
in – in or into	Ich gehe **in die** Stadt. I'm going into town.	Ich bin **in der** Stadt. I am in town.
neben – next to	Wir fahren **neben ein** Kaufhaus. We are driving near to a department store.	Wir wohnen **neben einem** Kaufhaus. We live near to a department store.

2 The same rule applies to **über** (over), **unter** (under) and **vor** (in front of).

Q Make up two sentences for each of the prepositions über, unter and vor, one using the accusative and the other using the dative.

See page 49 for other prepositions

Education

THE BARE BONES

➤ You will probably have to write a letter, e-mail, fax or message in the exam. Be sure that you know what each of these looks like and follow the right form.

➤ You may see some German handwriting in the exam. Don't let it put you off. It is different, but not enormously!

A Differences in schools

READ

1 <u>Welcher Satz beschreibt Schüler von welchem Land?</u>
Which sentence describes pupils from which country?

Q What are the differences between schools in Great Britain and Germany?

a Ich trage keine Uniform. Ich kann für die Schule anziehen, was ich will.

b Ich habe nur morgens Schule. Nachmittags habe ich immer frei.

c Die Schule beginnt ungefähr um neun Uhr und endet um halb vier.

d Ich bekomme meine Schulbücher und Hefte kostenlos von meinem Lehrer.

e Nachmittags kann man Sport treiben oder an anderen Aktivitäten teilnehmen.

B Problems at school and reasons for study

SPEAK

1 <u>Beantworte die Fragen mit möglichst viel Information.</u>
Answer the questions with as much information as possible.

Beispiel:

• *Warum studierst du Mathematik?*

- *Ich studiere Mathematik, weil ich das Fach wichtig finde.*

Remember
Write notes to help you. You can also write out the answer in full, read it out loud, then try to remember it without looking.

> Warum studierst du Informatik?

> Warum lernst du Deutsch?

> Warum hast du deine Hausaufgaben nicht gemacht?

> Warum siehst du so müde aus?

> Warum warst du gestern nicht in der Schule?

> Gefällt dir die Schule?

C About your education

1 Lies den Brief.
Read the letter.

Bad Marienberg, den 17. Januar

Lieber Greg,

Ich möchte dir ein bisschen über meine Schule erzählen. Ich besuche die Realschule Bad Marienberg. Die Schule ist ganz klein mit ungefähr 200 Schülern!

In der Schule gibt es eine Bibliothek, ein Schwimmbad, einen grossen Schulhof, ein Büro für den Schulleiter, ein Lehrerzimmer und eine kleine Sporthalle. Die Lehrer sind im allgemeinen sehr nett. Ich mag am liebsten den Schulleiter, Herr Am Zehnhof. Ich bin in meiner Schule sehr glücklich.

Nach der Schule habe ich vor, bei meinen Eltern in ihrem Geschäft zu arbeiten. Ich lerne so viel wie möglich, damit ich es später anwenden kann. Ich lerne Englisch, so dass ich mit Kunden diskutieren kann. Ich lerne Mathematik, um beim Rechnen keine Probleme zu haben. Schließlich ist Informatik für das Geschäft sehr wichtig.

Wie ist deine Schule? Wie ist das Gebäude? Und die Lehrer? Gefällt dir die Schule? Was möchtest du nach der Schule machen?

Schreibe mir bald.

Dein

Jonas

2 Schreibe einen Brief an Jonas. Beantworte die Fragen, die im Brief stehen. (150–200 Wörter)
Write a letter to Jonas. Be sure to answer all the questions from the letter. (150–200 words)

From your letter to Jonas, learn some phrases about your school.

PRACTICE

1 Ask a friend to interview you about your school.

- Wie ist deine Schule?
- Hast du die Schule gern?
- Warst du früher an einer anderen Schule?
- Wie war diese Schule?
- Was möchtest du nach der Schule machen?
- Was möchtest du später werden?

If you are not sure how to pronounce something, ask your teacher or your language assistant. Practise until you can say it with confidence.

THE BARE BONES

➤ You may have to talk about your dream job, your part-time job, jobs of friends or members of your family.

➤ Using the future tense is particularly relevant in this topic area. Remember you can use the simple future (Grammar page 25) if you are not fully confident with using <u>werden</u> (Grammar page 25, 43).

A What's my line?

WRITE

1 <u>Beschreibe die folgenden Berufe ohne die Berufsbezeichnung zu nennen!</u>
Describe these jobs without mentioning the name.

Beispiel:

Ich habe Kontakt mit Kindern von 6 bis 18 Jahren in diesem Beruf. Ich unterrichte in einer Schule. (Antwort = Lehrer)

Verkäufer   Taxifahrer   Briefträger   Bäcker   Zahnarzt   Stewardess

B Important characteristics for employees

READ

1 <u>Hier ist ein Diagramm. Lies die Information und beantworte die Fragen.</u>
Here is a graph. Read the information and answer the following questions.

Remember
You may be given a diagram or graph to interpret. Look at the task first – the answer may be very obvious and not need detailed study of the diagram!

Q Which of these qualities is most important, in your opinion? Why?

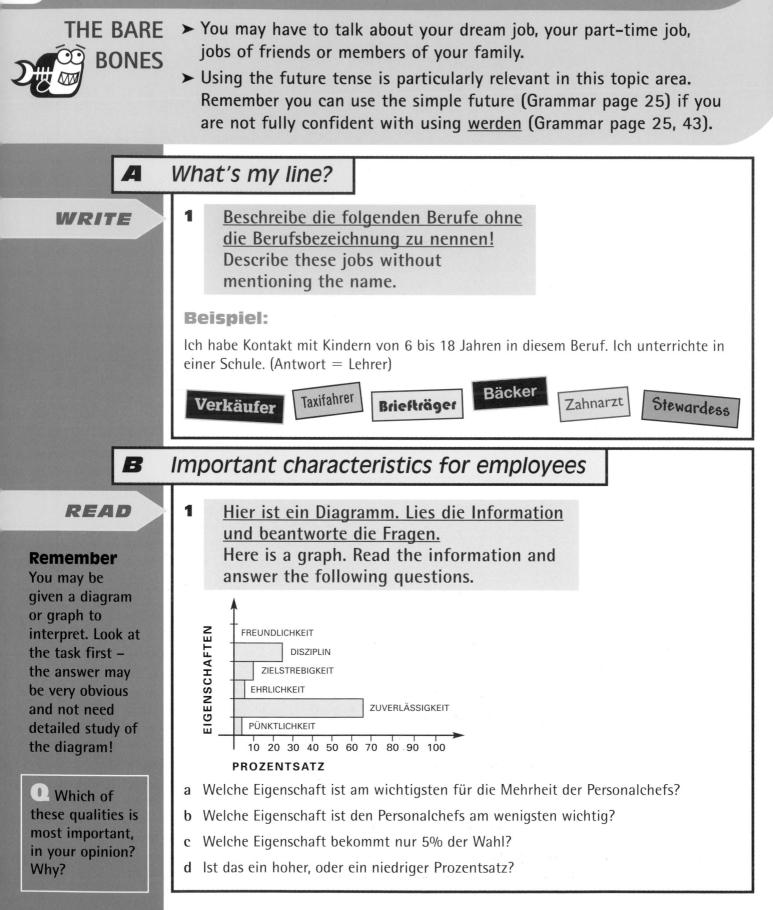

a Welche Eigenschaft ist am wichtigsten für die Mehrheit der Personalchefs?

b Welche Eigenschaft ist den Personalchefs am wenigsten wichtig?

c Welche Eigenschaft bekommt nur 5% der Wahl?

d Ist das ein hoher, oder ein niedriger Prozentsatz?

C Future plans

SPEAK

Remember
A good way to learn spoken text is to record yourself saying it. Listen to it over and over again, trying to predict words, sentences and eventually the whole thing!

Q Give reasons for wanting to do the jobs listed in Question A1.

1 Verbinde den richtigen Beruf mit der richtigen Erklärung.
Match the right job to the right explanation.

Beispiel:

Ich möchte später Musiker werden, weil ich Musik liebe.

1 weil ich mich sehr gut mit Kindern verstehe.

a Manager/in

4 weil ich eine geborene Führungspersönlichkeit bin.

b Informatiker/in

2 weil ich sehr organisiert und diszipliniert bin.

c Sekretär/in

5 weil ich gut mit Computern umgehen kann.

d Lehrer/in

3 weil ich mich gerne in andere Personen verwandle.

e Schauspieler/in

2 Was möchtest du später werden und warum?
What do you want to do when you are older and why?

PRACTICE

1 Write a text pretending to be Anja, explaining what you want to do and why.

Anja:

- wants to be a professional sportswoman
- swims very well
- is disciplined and strong
- would like to become a world champion
- knows that study is important so will work hard to get her Abitur
- wants to find a good trainer who will give her time to do schoolwork.

Never leave an answer line blank in the exam. Even if you are not 100% sure, it's better to have a go than not write anything!

world champion = die Weltmeisterin
trainer = der Trainer

Vocabulary

A Education

Ich trage keine Uniform. Ich kann für die Schule anziehen, was ich will.	I don't wear a uniform. I can wear what I like to school.
Ich habe nur morgens Schule. Nachmittags habe ich immer frei.	I only have school in the mornings. In the afternoon I am always free.
Die Schule beginnt ungefähr um neun Uhr und ist um halb vier aus.	School begins at about 9am and finishes at about 3.30pm.
Ich bekomme meine Schulbücher und Hefte kostenlos von meinem Lehrer.	I get my school books free of charge from my teacher.
Ich esse das Mittagessen mit meinen Freunden in der Schulkantine.	I have lunch with my friends in the school canteen.
Mit achtzehn werde ich die Schule verlassen.	I will leave school at eighteen.

das Abitur	A Level equivalent	das Gymnasium	secondary school (grammar)
die Ausbildung	training	die Hochschule	university
die Berufsausbildung	training for a job	der Kindergarten	nursery
die Fachhochschule	polytechnic	der Lehrling	apprentice
die Gesamtschule	secondary school (comprehensive)	das Pflichtfach	obligatory subject
die Grundschule	primary school	die Realschule	secondary school
		das Resultat	result

B Careers and future plans

Ich möchte später Tennisspieler werden.	I want to be a tennis player when I'm older.

der/die Bäcker/in	baker	die Pünktlichkeit	punctuality
der/die Briefträger/in	postman	der/die Sänger/in	singer
die Disziplin	discipline	der Steward	steward
die Ehrlichkeit	truthfulness	die Stewardess	stewardess
die Freundlichkeit	friendliness	der/die Taxifahrer/in	taxi driver
der/die Fußballspieler/in	football player	der Tourismus	tourism
		die Verantwortung	responsibility
der Handel	business/dealing	der/die Verkäufer/in	salesman/woman
der Krankenpfleger	male nurse	der/die Zahnarzt/ Zahnärztin	dentist
die Krankenschwester	female nurse		
der Lohn	salary	zielstrebig	goal focused
das Marketing	marketing	die Zuverlässigkeit	dependability

Grammar

C Questions

Remember
When you answer a question about yourself, make sure you change the ending of the verb. With **ich** the ending is almost always –e.

1 You ask questions in German by changing the sentence around.

Du wohnst in Deutschland. is a statement – 'You live in Germany.'

Wohnst du in Deutschland? is a question – 'Do you live in Germany?'

2 The same thing happens after question words.

Wo wohnst du?

Was studierst du?

Warum machst du das?

Wer wohnt mit dir?

Wann gehst du aus?

Wie kommst du zur Schule?

Wieviele CDs hast du?

D Pronouns

1 Words that are used instead of nouns are called pronouns. They change depending on their role in a sentence.

subject (nominative)	ich	Ich heiße Michael.	du	Du bist dreizehn.
object (accusative)	mich	Er ruft **mich** an.	dich	Er hat **dich** gesehen.
dative	mir	Gib es **mir**.	dir	Ich schicke **dir** eine Karte.

Q Answer all the questions in the grid above about yourself.

2 A similar pattern works with **er**, **sie** and **es**.

subject (nominative)	object (accusative)	dative
er	ihn	ihm
sie	sie	ihr
es	es	ihm

Q Put the correct pronoun in the gaps.

(meine Katze)
_____ ist klein.

(der Brief) Ich habe _____ geschickt.

(meine Mutter) Ich gehe mit _____ einkaufen.

Er war in der Stadt. Ich habe **ihn** gesehen.
Er weinte. Ich gab **ihm** einen Tafel Schokolade.

Sie war zu Hause. Ich habe **sie** angerufen.
Sie wollte gehen. Ich gab **ihr** meine Eintrittskarte.

Es war nicht teuer. Ich habe **es** gekauft.
Das Kind war krank, ich gab **ihm** Tabletten.

3 The prepositions which change the words **der**, **die**, **das**, **ein**, **eine** or **ein** change pronouns too!

Ich gehe **mit ihm** einkaufen. Wo ist mein Stuhl? Ich sitze **auf ihm!**

Job applications

THE BARE BONES

➤ Official forms, such as ID forms, application forms, booking requests or CVs, feature fairly frequently in the exam.

➤ Look for key words. You don't have to understand every word to answer the question.

➤ Being able to use the telephone is an important skill. It may be part of your spoken exam or be included in the written exam.

A Writing a CV

WRITE

1 Lies die Informationen. Fülle die Lücken aus.
Read the CV headings and the details. Fill in the gaps.

LEBENSLAUF

Name: _____

Alter: _____

Geburtsdatum: _____

Adresse: _____

Telefonnummer: _____

Schulbildung: _____

Hobbys: _____

Tiere, Umweltschutz, Lesen, Schwimmen

17

Scherer, Elisabeth

Feigenberg 26, 6729 Hatzenbühl

07275 2425

1987–1992 Grundschule in Jockgrim

1992–2000 Goethe-Gymnasium, Wörth

seit 2000 – Universität Trier

9. Oktober 1981

B Telephoning about a job

SPEAK

1 Lies die Anzeigen und ruf die Firmen an.
Read the adverts and call the companies.

- Give your name, address and phone number.
- Say what you are interested in and why.
- Say what experience you can offer.

GESUCHT

freundlich/
höflich/selbstsicher
Für die Rezeption in einer
Werbeagentur.

Hamburg 22 34 56 54 Telefax: 22 34 56 56

WIR SUCHEN … JOURNALIST

Interesse für Neuigkeiten?
Bewusstsein für alles Aktuelles?
Intelligenter? Schreibestil? Lebenslauf
und Arbeitsproben schicken.

Fernmeldstrasse 18, 67399 Jockgrim.

Ich interessiere mich für …   Ich habe die Anzeige … gesehen.

Kann ich bitte mit jemandem von der Personalabteilung sprechen?

Kann ich bitte eine Nachricht hinterlassen? Wäre es bitte möglich mit … zu sprechen?

Q Describe your telephone call in the past tense (e.g.

Ich habe … angerufen.

Ich habe gesagt, dass …).

C CV letter

READ

Remember
The questions will be in the same order as the information appears in the text. Work your way through the questions one at a time, finding the answer in the text.

Remember
Don't be put off by long words. They're often just two shorter words put together, like Telefon + Nummer = Telefonnummer!

Q Write your own CV. Write out the headings first without help, then check them.

1 Lies den Lebenslauf.
Read the CV.

LEBENSLAUF

Ich heiße Marla Friedhof. Ich bin am 29. August 1985 in Dresden geboren. Meine Staatsangehörigkeit ist deutsch. Ich habe einen Bruder und eine Schwester. Zur Zeit wohne ich in München. Meine Adresse ist Kaiserdamm 45, 8350 München. Die Telefonnummer ist 0810 87 90 42. Von 1987 bis 1992 besuchte ich die Grundschule in der Stadtmitte Dresden. Seit 1992 besuche ich das Schiller-Gymnasium in München. Ich mache gerade mein Abitur in den Fächern Mathematik, Physik, Deutsch und Geschichte. Meine Hobbys sind Computer und Lesen. Ich möchte später gern Informatikerin werden.

2 Beantworte die Fragen.
Answer the questions.

a Wie ist ihr Name?

b Was ist ihr Geburtsdatum?

c Wo ist ihr Geburtsort?

d Wie viele Geschwister hat sie?

e Wie ist ihre Adresse?

f Was machte sie von 1987 bis 1992?

g Was macht sie jetzt?

h Was ist ihr Berufswunsch?

PRACTICE

1 Write a letter to your penpal saying:

- what you'd like to be when you're older
- what you're interested in
- what your favourite subjects are
- what your parents do.

You may be asked to write up to 150 words. Practise writing longer passages – you need to know what 100 words looks like!

Social issues

THE BARE BONES

➤ If there is something unusual about your life which you would like to mention in the exam, make sure you learn any words you need to be able to talk or write about it.

➤ Remember you don't **have** to give true information about yourself. You can make it all up if you wish!

A Family arrangements

WRITE

1 <u>Lies diese Anzeige für einen Brieffreund.</u>
Read this advert for a penpal.

Remember
You may have to make a short, spoken presentation, as well as doing role-plays and general conversation.

> Brieffreund gesucht!
>
> Ich bin ein fünfzehnjähriger Schüler mit besonderen Lebensumständen. Während der Woche wohne ich bei meiner Mutter und ihrem Freund in Wien; Wochenenden aber verbringe ich in einem Dorf in der Nähe bei meinem Vater und seiner neuen Frau.
>
> Ist deine Familie auch außergewöhnlich? Auf welche Weise? Wie gehst du damit um? Schreibe mir, Lukas, Chiffre Nummer 14.

2 <u>Schreibe eine Anzeige.</u>
Write an advert.

Stefanie 13 yrs

- lives with her grandmother and two brothers in Frankfurt

Would like to share experiences with someone in a similar situation.

B The law and young people

SPEAK

1 <u>Wann darf man ...?</u>
When are you allowed to ...?

14 **15** **16** **18**

... in den Schulferien arbeiten

... mit der Erlaubnis der Eltern heiraten

... in der Öffentlichkeit rauchen

... ein Mofa/Moped/Auto fahren

... ohne Erlaubnis heiraten

... wählen

... alkoholische Getränke in einer Bar/einem Restaurant trinken und kaufen

Beispiel:

Mit 14 darf man in den Schulferien arbeiten.

Man muss 14 sein, um in den Schulferien zu arbeiten.

B

2 <u>Wie findest du das?</u>
What do you think about that?

Das finde ich	ein bisschen	widersprüchlich.
	ziemlich	sinnvoll.
	ganz	doof.
	total	gefährlich.
	überhaupt nicht	komisch.
	nicht besonders	intelligent.

C *Leaving home*

READ

1 <u>Lies den Text und beantworte die Fragen – richtig oder falsch?</u>
Read the text and answer the questions – true or false?

Die Mehrheit der deutschen Jugendlichen lebt bei Mama und Papa. Dabei sind es meistens die jungen Männer, die länger im Elternhaus bleiben: von den 25jährigen wohnt immerhin noch fast ein Drittel im »Hotel Mutti«. Der meistgenannte Grund: »Zu Hause ist es einfach bequemer«. 25 Prozent aller Jugendlichen in Deutschland leben jedoch bei nur einem Elternteil (das ist fast immer die Mutter).

		richtig	falsch
a	Die meisten deutschen Jugendlichen wohnen bei ihren Eltern.		
b	Mädchen bleiben länger zu Hause bei den Eltern.		
c	30 Prozent aller Männer über 25 wohnen im Hotel.		
d	Ein Viertel aller Jugendlichen lebt bei der Mutter.		

Q Rewrite any incorrect answers.

PRACTICE

1 Prepare a 1–2 minute presentation about your life at home.

- Start with 'Ich werde über meine Familie und mein Haus sprechen'.
- Include information about your family: names, ages, jobs.
- Describe your house and say what you think of it.
- Say what you think your brothers/sisters/you will do in the future.
- Describe where your parents lived before.

In the role-play there will usually be a problem to solve (e.g. if booking a hotel room, perhaps there is no Zimmer mit Bad, only mit Dusche!).

Vocabulary

A Job applications

Sind Sie zuverlässig und diszipliniert?	*Are you reliable and disciplined?*
Sind Sie freundlich und voller Initiative?	*Are you friendly and full of initiative?*
Haben Sie ... bis ... Stunden pro Woche übrig?	*Do you have between ... and ... spare hours per week?*
Möchten Sie Ihre Karriere im ... entwickeln?	*Would you like to develop your career in ...?*
Bitte Lebenslauf an diese Adresse schicken.	*Please send your CV to this address.*
Ich interessiere mich für ...	*I'm interested in ...*
Ich habe die Anzeige in ... gesehen.	*I saw the advert in ...*
Kann ich bitte mit jemandem von der Personalabteilung sprechen?	*Please could I speak to someone from the personnel department?*

das Alter	*age*	der Lebenslauf	*CV*
das Geburtsdatum	*date of birth*	die Schulbildung	*education*
der Geburtsort	*place of birth*	die Staatsangehörigkeit	*nationality*

Von 1987 bis 1992 besuchte ich die Grundschule/das Gymnasium in ...	*From 1987 to 1992 I went to primary school/grammar school in ...*
Ich mache gerade mein Abitur in den Fächern ...	*I am doing my A levels in ... (list subjects)*
Meine Hobbys sind ...	*My hobbies are ...*
Ich möchte später gern ... werden.	*When I'm older I would like to be ...*

B Social issues

Wann darf man in den Schulferien arbeiten?	*When are you allowed to work in the school holidays?*
mit der Erlaubnis der Eltern	*with your parents' agreement*
in der Öffentlichkeit rauchen	*to smoke in public*
Ich bin ein fünfzehnjähriger Schüler mit besonderen Lebensumständen.	*I am a fifteen-year-old student with unusual living circumstances.*
Ich suche jemanden, mit dem ich diese Erfahrung teilen kann.	*I am looking for someone to share this experience with.*
Ist deine Familie auch außergewöhnlich?	*Is your family unusual too?*
Auf welche Weise?	*In what way?*
Wie gehst du damit um?	*How do you cope with that?*

arbeitslos	*unemployed*	der Krebs	*cancer*
alkoholische Getränke	*alcoholic drinks*	sich gewöhnen an	*to get used to*
die Drogen	*drugs*	sinnvoll	*sensible*
der/die Drogensüchtige	*drug addict*	wählen	*to vote*
gefährlich	*dangerous*	die Werbung	*advert*
komisch	*funny*	widersprüchlich	*contradictory*
die Krankheit	*illness*	die Zigarette	*cigarette*

Grammar

C More past tense

1 We have seen that most verbs in the perfect tense begin with **ge-** and end in **-en** or **-t**. There are some which are different.

2 Verbs that end in **-ieren** or start with **er-**, **ver-**, or **be-** do not have a past participle with **ge-**:

Ich habe ein Zimmer **reserviert**.
I have reserved a room.

Wir haben eine Woche in Frankfurt **verbracht**.
We spent a week in Frankfurt.

Ich habe Berlin **besucht**.
I visited Berlin.

3 Some other common verbs have irregular past participles. There is probably a list in your dictionary or text book. These include:

Wir haben unsere Bücher **gelesen**. We read our books.
Er hat **ferngesehen**. He watched TV.

4 In a sentence, the past participle (the part which normally begins with **ge-**) goes to the end.

Ich habe eine Katze **gekauft**. Ich habe Fußball **gespielt**.

5 Sometimes, when a word like **weil** or **als** is used, the part of **haben** or **sein** which goes with the past participle goes right to the end, after the past participle.

Er war böse, weil ich nicht gespielt **habe**.
Wir waren unterwegs, als er mir die Geschichte erzählt **hat**.

Q Write sentences in the past tense, saying what you did on your last holiday and why.

Learn seven or eight past participles and make sure you can use them confidently. Once you are using them, you can start adding to your collection!

Listening exam practice

- The following pages will give you some listening practice.
- Use the video or your own recording from the television to do the activities.
- At first you can pause, rewind and replay your tape as much as you need to help you answer the questions.
- As you get better and better, you can just play each part once, then pause the tape to write your answers and play it one more time to check. This is just how the tape is played in your exam.

A Favourite subjects at school

Remember
If you get a question like this in the exam, read the words on the exam paper before the tape is played.

1 Let's have a look at the pupils from the video and their favourite school subjects. The question asked is: **Was sind deine Lieblingsfächer?**

2 Before you watch the video, make a list (in German!) of which subjects you think the pupils like best.

3 Now listen to the pupils and check their subjects against your list.

4 <u>Welche Fächer mögen sie auch? Hör zu. Kreuze die Fächer an, die du auf der Aufnahme hörst.</u>
Which other subjects do pupils like? Listen and tick the school subjects you hear on the tape.

☐ Biologie ☐ Informatik ☐ Musik ☐ Politik ☐ Chemie ☐ Kunst
☐ Physik ☐ Sport ☐ Erdkunde ☐ Latein ☐ Spanisch ☐ Theater

B Subjects you don't like

1 The pupils were also asked which subjects they don't like: **Welche Fächer magst du nicht?**

2 Which subjects do you think they like least? Before you listen, write a list of subjects that you'd expect the pupils to dislike.

3 <u>Welche Fächer mögen die Schüler nicht? Hör zu und schreibe die Fächer neben den richtigen Namen.</u>
Which subjects do the pupils not like? Listen and write the subjects next to each name.

Q Do you recognise all the school subjects that are mentioned on the tape? If not, check the unfamiliar ones!

Austen: _____ Irina: _____ Simon: _____

Ivanka: _____ Svenja: _____ Natalie: _____

Stefan: _____

C Getting up for school

1 When do you get up in the morning? **Wann stehst du auf?**

2 Look at the clocks below and work out the German for the times in your head.

3 When you watch the tape, tick the boxes by the times you hear.

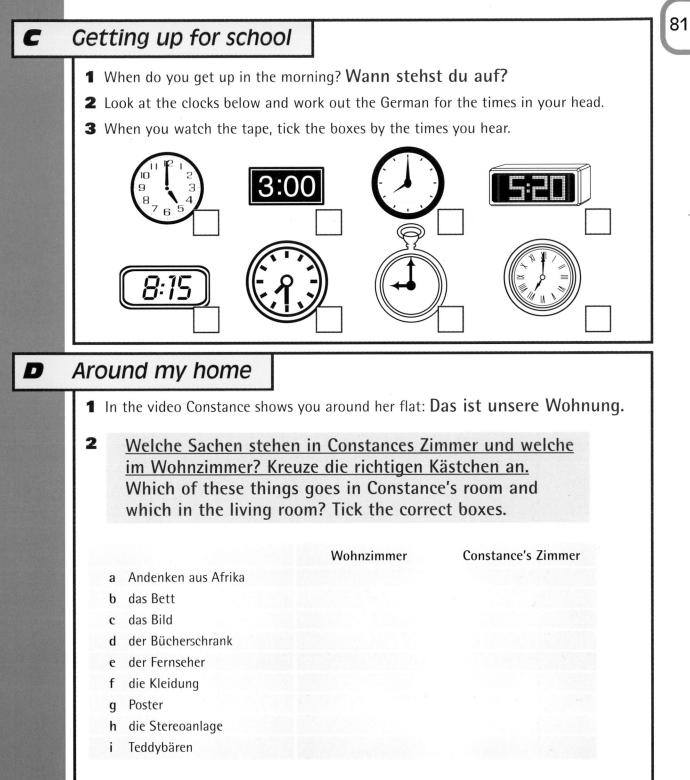

D Around my home

1 In the video Constance shows you around her flat: **Das ist unsere Wohnung.**

2 <u>Welche Sachen stehen in Constances Zimmer und welche im Wohnzimmer? Kreuze die richtigen Kästchen an.</u>
Which of these things goes in Constance's room and which in the living room? Tick the correct boxes.

	Wohnzimmer	Constance's Zimmer
a Andenken aus Afrika		
b das Bett		
c das Bild		
d der Bücherschrank		
e der Fernseher		
f die Kleidung		
g Poster		
h die Stereoanlage		
i Teddybären		

3 Play the tape again to check your answers.

E Healthy living

1 <u>Was ist gesund und was ungesund? Kreuze die Kästchen an.</u>
Which of these is healthy and which unhealthy? Tick the boxes.

		gesund	nicht gesund
a	Bonbons		
b	Drogen		
c	Fleisch		
d	Gemüse		
e	Hamburger		
f	Nudeln		
g	Obst		
h	Pommes frites		
i	Rauchen		
j	Schokolade		
k	Sport		
l	Süßigkeiten		
m	Vitamine		

2 Now watch the tape and check your answers with the suggestions from the video.

F Food

1 In this activity you are going to identify which foods the two people in the video are eating.

2 Check the list below. Even if you don't understand the words, say them quietly to yourself so you will recognise them when you hear them.

3 <u>Was isst die Frau und was isst der Mann?</u>
<u>Kreuze die richtige Person an.</u>
What do they eat? Tick the right person for each item.

	Frau	Mann
Pommes frites		
Wiener Schnitzel		
Kartoffelsalat		
Würstchen		
gemischter Salat		

4 Can you remember what the woman was drinking?

Remember

In listening activities, if you read the words on the paper quietly to yourself, they will be easier to understand when you hear them.

Q Ask a friend to read out twenty food items in German. Can you understand all of them? You can then do the same for your friend.

G Describing your family

1 In the video, Rolli asks his friends if they've got any brothers and sisters:
Hast du Geschwister?

2 Who says the following? You're listening for specific information here, so concentrate and remember who's speaking each time!

a Ich habe keine Geschwister.   Miriam ☐
b Ich habe eine Schwester.   Marko ☐
c Ich habe vier Brüder.   Jessica ☐
d Ich habe einen Bruder und eine Schwester. Esther ☐
e Ich habe einen Bruder.   Thomas ☐

3 Sonja talks to more teenagers about their brothers and sisters.

Hör zu und verbinde die richtigen Namen mit der richtigen Familieninformation.

Listen and write down how many brothers and sisters each teenager has.

Ivanka _____
Christopher _____
Katrin _____
Irina _____
Nada _____
Stefan _____
Cecilia _____
Ulrike _____
Sabine _____
Michael _____

4 Christopher, Irina and Constance describe their brothers and sisters in more detail. Listen again and fill in these three ID cards.

Constances Bruder: ....
Alter: ....
Haare: ....
Augen: ....
Größe: ....

Irinas Bruder: ....
Alter: ....
Haare: ....
Er ist: ....

Christophers Bruder: ....
Alter: ....
Haare: ....
Augen: ....
Er ist: ....

Q Say how many brothers and sisters you have and describe them. Can you understand someone else giving the same information about their family?

H Holiday activities

1 Sonja is visiting Mittenwald, a holiday resort in the German Alps. She asks what there is to do there in winter and summer: **Was kann man hier im Winter/im Sommer machen?**

2 What do you think you can do in the winter and summer there? Write two lists, choosing from the words below.

Bergsteigen   Eisstockschießen   Fallschirmspringen   Kajak fahren
Klettern   Mountainbike fahren   Rodeln   Schlittschuhlaufen
Schwimmen   Skilaufen   Wandern

3 Now listen to check your answers.

I Arranging to go out

1 And finally, let's look at how to arrange a meeting. First, listen to Jessica and Miriam and answer the two questions below.
   a Wo treffen sie sich?   b Wann treffen sie sich?

2 Now listen to Nico arranging to meet Elke.
   a Wohin gehen sie?   b Wann treffen sie sich?

J Asking for directions

Remember
A good way to prepare for the listening is to say any words you see on the exam paper quietly to yourself. This will help you to remember when the tape is playing.

1 Wind forward to the section about Berlin. In the video, some people are asking for directions: **Wie komme ich zum/zur ...?**

2 Hör zu. Verbinde die Fragen (links) mit den richtigen Antworten (rechts).
Listen and then join the questions on the left with the answers on the right.

1 Zum Reichstag?   a mit der U-Bahn
2 Zum Zoo?   b zu Fuß durch den Tiergarten
3 Zum Fernsehturm?   c mit dem Bus Nummer 100
4 Zum Brandenburger Tor?   d zu Fuß bis zur Karl-Marx-Allee

3 Did you read those questions and answers before you listened to the video?

K Getting to school

Q Can you ask for directions and understand the answer? Try it with a map and some friends.

1 **Wie kommst du zur Schule?** Christopher and his friends tell Sonja how they get to school. Which mode of transport do you think most of them use – and which one don't they use?

mit dem Auto ☐   mit der Bahn ☐   mit dem Bus und der Bahn ☐
mit dem Fahrrad ☐   zu Fuß ☐

2 Listen (**hör zu**) and check your answers by writing the words above in order of popularity (1–5) with the most popular as number 1.

L Travelling around

1 Wolfgang's on his way to see a friend. He's buying a ticket for his journey.

2 <u>Hör zu und unterstreiche die richtigen Sätze.</u>
Listen and then underline the right phrases.

1 Wolfgang fährt mit:
  a dem Bus b dem Zug c der U-Bahn.
2 Die Fahrkarte kostet:
  a 1,30 DM b 3,70 DM c 5,00 DM.
3 Er nimmt die Linie:
  a 2 b 22 c 12.

M Buying tickets

1 Nico is at the main station (**der Hauptbahnhof**) in Cologne. Where's he going? What kind of ticket does he buy?

2 <u>Hör zu und kreuze die richtigen Sätze an.</u>
Listen and tick the phrases which are right.

a eine Fahrkarte nach Düsseldorf   eine Fahrkarte nach Amsterdam
b für heute   für morgen
c einfach   hin und zurück
d kostet 74,20 DM   kostet 85,20 DM

N What is your job?

1 Olaf and Rüdiger both work in television. Read the statements below. Underline any words you don't know. You could check them in a dictionary before you watch the video.

2 <u>Welche Sätze sind richtig und welche sind falsch?</u>
<u>Kreuze die richtigen Sätze an.</u>
Which statements are correct and which are not?
Tick only the correct ones.

		richtig
a	Olaf ist Moderator von Beruf.	
b	Er hat keine Ausbildung gemacht.	
c	Er findet seinen Beruf langweilig.	
d	50 Prozent seiner Kollegen sind Frauen.	
e	Rüdiger ist Toningenieur von Beruf.	
f	Er hat Sport und Informatik studiert.	
g	Sein Beruf ist eine Mischung aus Technik und Musik.	
h	Man muss für diesen Beruf musikalisch sein.	

O On the phone

1 Nico is practising his phone skills with Elke. Read their phone conversation. Put the phrases in the right order.
a Danke. Auf Wiederhören.
b Ja, gut.
c Guten Tag. Könnte ich bitte mit Frau Maier sprechen?
d Könnte sie mich zurückrufen? – 44 63?
e Sie ist nicht da.
f Apparat Frau Schneider, guten Tag!

2 Now listen to check your answers. You're only listening for the gist of the conversation at the moment, so you don't have to understand every word. In the next activity, you'll be listening for specific details, so you'll have to concentrate harder.

3 Hör noch einmal zu. Unterstreiche die richtigen Sätze.
Listen to Nico's phone call again and underline (unterstreiche) the right phrases.

1 When Nico answered the phone, what did he forget to say?
a seinen Vornamen   b seinen Nachnamen

2 Who's on the other line?
a Frau Hilger   b Frau Maier

3 What's the number of the caller?
a 40 63   b 44 63

4 Nico asks the caller to repeat. But what else does he say?
a Sprechen Sie bitte langsamer.   b Das weiß ich nicht.

5 When will Frau Maier be back?
a Sie ist um 10 Uhr wieder da.   b Sie ist gegen 2 Uhr wieder da.

6 Did you remember to read the phrases before you played the video to help you focus?

7 Now listen to check your answers.

Q On the phone, could you understand someone who wanted to leave their name and a simple message? Practise with a friend.

P In the bank

1 In the video, Nico goes to the bank to pick up some money for his boss.

2 Hör zu. Kreuze die richtigen Sätze an.
Listen to Nico at the bank and tick the corrrect phrases.

1 What currency does Nico want?
a englisches Geld   b ausländisches Geld

2 What other items, apart from Frau Maier's passport, does Nico show?
a ihre Scheckkarte und einen Reisescheck   b ihre Scheckkarte und eine Vollmacht

3 How much money did Frau Maier order?
a 200 Pfund   b 2000 DM

4 What does the bank clerk say to Nico?
a Das machen wir normalerweise nicht.   b Das geht in Ordnung.

Q Do you know all your German numbers? It is especially important to understand higher numbers in this sort of situation.

P

5 How does Nico reply?
 a Frau Maier kommt sofort.   b Frau Maier kann nicht.

6 What else does the bank clerk want to see?
 a Nicos Ausweis   b Nicos Scheckkarte

Q Your dream holiday

1 Sonja asked some people about their dream holiday: **Was ist Ihr Traumurlaub?** What do you think the favourite destinations are? Read the list below and choose eight of the most likely ones.

Amerika	die Antarktis	Australien und Neuseeland	Belgien
der Dschungel	Hawaii	Holland (die Niederlande)	Finnland
Kanada	die Karibik	Polen	Sibirien
eine Weltreise	die Wüste		

2 Now listen and check your answers.

3 Write down your own 'Top 5' list of ideal holiday destinations.

R Around Berlin

1 In the next bit, Esther shows you round 'her' part of Berlin. Careful – you're listening for specific information here, so concentrate hard.

2 Lies die Fragen und unterstreiche die richtigen Sätze.
 Read the questions and underline the right phrases.

1 Esther wohnt in:
 a Köln b Kreuzberg.

2 Sie trifft ihre:
 a Freundinnen b Klassenkameraden.

3 In Kreuzberg gibt es viele:
 a Kirchen, Kneipen, Gebäude
 b Cafés, Clubs, Geschäfte.

4 Viele der Geschäfte sind:
 a deutsch b türkisch.

5 Es gibt aber auch:
 a wenig Kriminalität b viele Probleme.

6 Esther findet Kreuzberg:
 a sehr interessant
 b ziemlich international.

PRACTICE

When you've got a spare moment, put the German Bitesize video on and play a clip that you find particularly interesting – or one that covers the topic area you're revising at the time. Listen and watch the clip through once and note down any key words you'd like to learn. Then rewind the tape and play the clip again – but this time with the volume turned right down. Pause the tape every so often and say a sentence or phrase to describe what you can see or what's happening. Then carry on like this, pausing and speaking and then continuing.

You can then watch the clip again at the end with the volume turned up and see how much you remember or compare the things that you said with the actual German speakers.

Listening-exam practice

- There are many different task types in the listening exam.
- You have already met a number of them in the listening section.
- Here are some more examples for you to practise.
- Each clip has a series of tips to help you complete it, the question as it might appear in an exam and a completed answer.
- You may feel confident enough to just do the task without the tips and then use the completed answer to check your work, or you may want to read the tips and check the answer before trying it yourself.
- Use this practice section in the way that works best for you.

A Things to do in Hamburg

From Unit 4.

Find the clip where Austen and his friends speak about what you can do in Hamburg.

> **TIPS**
> - Look at the grid. Which words can't you recognise? What might they mean? Spend some time looking at them and say them quietly to yourself.
> - Are the words you didn't understand die Alster, Blankenese, die Elbe and St. Pauli? These are all rivers and districts in Hamburg, so you won't find them in a dictionary!
> - Can you work out by just looking at the activity what you might be expected to do? There are people's names at the top and a list of places in a town down the side.
> - The instructions say 'Who mentions which sights? Listen and tick the right names in the grid'. In the exam, you may not have an English translation, but would you be able to work out what to do anyway?

1 Wer spricht über welchen Sehenswürdigkeiten? Hör zu und kreuze die Namen an.

	Austen	Irina	Christopher	Constance	Julia	Cecilia
a die Alster						
b Blankenese						
c Einkaufspassagen						
d das Einkaufszentrum						
e die Elbe						
f der Hafen						
g der Fernsehturm						
h die Innenstadt						
i Kirchen						
j Museen						
k das Rathaus						
l die Speicherstadt						
m St. Pauli						

B What you like about where you live

Continued from the clip above (Unit 4).

> **TIPS**
> - In the listening exam, using your initiative can be very helpful.
> - A considerable amount of the following activity could be done without hearing the German!
> - Have a go at this activity before you watch the clip and see how much you would have got right.
> - You are going to be asked why you think Austen and his friends like living in Hamburg.
> - Read the statements below. Which ones do you think apply to Hamburg?
> - Use your common sense for this activity – you might know that Hamburg is a big German city, so you could tick the statements that apply to any big city.

1 Kreuze die richtigen Sätze an.

	Hamburg
a Man kann hier viel unternehmen.	
b Es ist hier langweilig.	
c Es ist eine schöne Stadt.	
d Hier ist viel los.	
e Die Luft ist hier sehr gut.	
f Hier gibt es viele Jugendliche.	
g Es ist sehr ruhig hier.	

2 Is there anything the young people don't like about Hamburg?

Read the three statements below and tick the right one.

> **TIP**
> - You can use your common sense again here – Hamburg is in the north of Germany, so choose the statement that is most likely.

a Es ist viel zu heiß.

b Das Wetter ist schlecht.

c Es regnet nie.

C What would you like to become?

From Unit 4.

Find the clip where Sonja asks her friends what they'd like to be later on in life:
Was möchtest du später werden?

> **TIPS**
>
> - Before you watch the video, have a quick think about the subject of jobs.
>   What sort of words do you think you might hear? What might the people say?
>
> - You are going to be asked to listen and tick the right boxes. If you look at the
>   activity, you would have known that already, right?

1   Hör zu und kreuze die richtigen Kästchen an.

		Nicole	Jan	Verena	Marco	Anna
a	Ärztin					
b	Geschäftsmann					
c	hat keine Ahnung					
d	Sängerin					
e	weiß nicht genau					

2   Did Nicole, Jan, Verena, Marco or Anna say the following things?

a   Ich weiß überhaupt nicht, was ich werden möchte.

b   Ich mag klassische Musik sehr gern.

c   Ich möchte gern Bücher schreiben.

d   Meine Mutter ist auch Ärztin.

e   Man ist unabhängig in diesem Beruf.

> **TIP**
>
> - Sometimes the words used on the tape are not exactly the same words you will
>   see in the exam paper. Don't let this panic you!
>
> - You won't always be given the information to choose from; you may have to
>   listen and write down what you hear.

D Television

From Unit 4.

Find the clips of TV adverts.

TIPS

- Don't panic! Activities like this might look scary and long, but once you start them, you'll be OK. Just take a deep breath, relax and tackle the activity bit by bit!

- Before you watch the video, look at the questions and see if you can work out what you will need to do. What sort of things will you hear?

- Use a dictionary if you're not sure of key words – but only look up four words at the most. Don't forget – you won't be able to use a dictionary in the exam.

- In this activity, you are being asked to listen and tick the right phrases for each advert.

---

1 Hör zu und kreuze die richtigen Sätze für die verbindete Werbung an.

---

1 Werbespot 1 ist für:

   a Kaffee.

   b Tee.

   c Kakao.

2 Werbespot 2 ist für:

   a Süßigkeiten mit Kräutern.

   b Kräutertee.

   c Käse mit Kräutern.

3 Im Produkt ist:

   a Zucker.

   b Zitrone.

   c Zimt.

4 Es kommt aus:

   a der Schweiz.

   b Italien.

   c Ungarn.

5 Werbespot 3 ist für:

   a ein pflanzliches Medikament.

   b Bonbons aus Kräutern.

   c Kinderschokolade.

6 Das Produkt gibt es:

   a im Supermarkt.

   b beim Arzt.

   c in der Apotheke.

7 Werbespot 4 ist:

   a für ein Frühstücksprodukt.

   b etwas zum Abendbrot.

   c für eine Zeitschrift.

8 Das Produkt kommt aus:

   a Deutschland.

   b der Schweiz.

   c Österreich.

E At the tourist office

From Unit 5.

Find the clip where Sonja is at the tourist office.

> **TIPS**
> - At the tourist office (**das Verkehrsamt**) in Hamburg, Sonja is asking for some information. What kind of things do you think she wants?
> - What do you think the assistant might give her? Make and read a list in German.

1 Hör Sonia zu. Was möchte sie? Schreibe es auf.

> **TIP**
> - Sonja is also asking for tips on what to see in Hamburg. Before you listen to the next bit, read the list below. Which would be suitable for a sunny day?

2 Welche Aktivitäten könnte man an einem sonnigen Tag machen? Kreuze die richtigen Antworten an.

	ein sonniger Tag
a im Café sitzen	
b das Einkaufszentrum besuchen	
c eine Hafenrundfahrt machen	
d auf den Fernsehturm gehen	
e Kirchen besichtigen	
f ins Museum gehen	
g eine Stadtrundfahrt mit dem Bus machen	

Now find the clip where Florian and Marco are asking tourists in Munich (**München**) what they've seen already and what they're doing tomorrow.

3 Wer spricht über welchen Sehenswürdigkeiten? Hör zu und kreuze die richtige Person an.

	Woman 1	Man 1	Girl	Man 2	Woman 2
a die City					
b Dachau					
c das Deutsche Museum					
d der Marienplatz					
e das Olympiastadion					
f Schwabing					
g der Viktualienmarkt					
h der Englische Garten					

4 Welche Sätze sind richtig?

		richtig
a	Die erste Touristin kommt aus Hamburg.	
b	Sie hat noch nicht viel von München gesehen.	
c	Der Mann aus Freiburg besucht heute das Deutsche Museum.	
d	Das junge Mädchen fährt morgen nach Schwabing.	
e	Der Tourist aus den USA ist erst seit heute in München.	
f	Die zweite Touristin will morgen den Marienplatz besuchen.	

Answers

A

1 Austen – f, g, j
   Irina – h, i
   Christopher – c, g
   Constance - g
   Julia – l
   Cecilia – a, b, d, f, g, k, m

B

1 a, c, d, f
2 b

C

1 a – Nicole, c – Jan, e – Verena, b – Marco, d – Anna
2 a – Jan, b – Anna, c – Verena, d – Nicole, e – Marco

D

1 1 – b, 2 – a, 3 – b, 4 – a, 5 – a, 6 – c, 7 – a, 8 – c

E

1 ein Stadtprospekt, ein alphabetisches Register, ein Stadtplan
2 c and d
3 Woman 1 – a;
   Man 1 – c, d;
   Girl – b, e, f;
   Man 2 –d;
   Woman 2 – g and h
4 a, e, f

Speaking-exam practice

- The speaking exam is generally made up of three parts: one or perhaps more role-plays, a presentation followed by discussion, and general conversation.

- In the Higher exam you will be expected to do a more difficult role-play, where you will probably have to react to an unexpected comment or question from the teacher/examiner. You will also be expected to speak for longer in discussion. Check the exact details with your teacher.

- The part of the speaking exam that carries the most marks is the general conversation. For this reason, the best practice you can do for this exam is to speak German as much and as often as possible, preferably with someone who speaks the language well and can correct you and help you develop your skills.

- The presentation is something you can prepare in considerable depth beforehand. You can also spend some time considering what the discussion following the presentation might be about and what questions you might be asked – you can prepare these too. It is also useful if you can get used to your voice being recorded.

- For the role-plays, you need to practise following instructions on a card and responding to the teacher/examiner. Your part of the role-play will tell you what to say. Some role-plays may give you more choice of what to say (as on the opposite page). Some, like the example below, require you to stick closely to what is given.

- If you are in a formal situation (shopping, buying tickets): use **Sie** for 'you'. If you are talking to a friend: use the familiar **du**.

Sample foundation role-play

Teacher's/examiner's role	Your card (model answer in brackets)
Guten Tag.	*Say you want a return ticket to Cologne.* (Ich möchte eine Fahrkarte nach Köln, hin und zurück.)
Ja, sicher.	*Ask how much it is.* (Wieviel kostet das?)
Fünfzig Euros.	*Ask what platform it leaves from.* (Wo fährt der Zug ab?)
Gleis 12.	*Ask where you can get a coffee.* (Wo kann ich eine Tasse Kaffee kaufen?)
Es gibt ein Café dort drüben.	*Say thank you.* (Vielen Dank.)

Sample higher role-play

These are more unstructured, and you will need to use a variety of tenses: past, present and future.

NB: The examiner is playing the role of your friend, so she/he will use **du** when speaking to you, and you should do the same!

Teacher's/examiner's role	Your card (model answer in brackets)
Wo warst du letztes Jahr auf Urlaub?	*Say where you went last year on holiday.* (Letztes Jahr sind wir nach der Schweiz gefahren, um meine Tante zu besuchen.)
Was machst du dieses Jahr?	*Say what you are going to do this year.* (Ich fahre mit einer Freundin nach Italien.)
Toll!	*Ask if he/she would like to spend the Easter holidays with you.* (Möchtest du die Osterferien bei mir in England verbringen?)
Vielen Dank, das wäre nett! Wie fahre ich denn am besten zu dir?	*Answer the question.* (Am besten fliegst du direkt nach Manchester, dann fährst du mit dem Zug nach Salford.)
Ich freue mich darauf!	

A Role-play 1 (Foundation level)

> **TIP**
> - If you can't remember a word, try another which gets across the same idea. If you can't remember the word for 'brochure', you could ask for information instead.

Teacher's/examiner's role

Guten Tag, kann ich Ihnen helfen?

Bitte schön.

Gehen Sie hier geradeaus. Nehmen Sie die erste Straße links und das Schwimmbad ist auf der linken Seite.

Um acht Uhr. Kommen Sie aus England?

Your card (model answer in brackets)

Say you'd like a brochure about the town.
(Ja, ich möchte eine Broschüre über München bitte.)

Ask how to get to the swimming pool.
(Können sie mir auch bitte erklären, wie mann zum Schwimmbad kommt?)

Ask what time it closes.
(Es schliesst um wieviel Uhr?)

Explain that you're here on holiday.
(Ja, ich bin hier auf Urlaub.)

B Role-play 2 (Foundation level)

> **TIP**
> - You're talking to a friend here, so use **du** for 'you'.

Your card (model answer in brackets)

Explain to your friend that you're thirsty.
(Ich habe Durst.)

Say what you want to drink.
(Ich möchte gern eine Limonade trinken.)

Say two things you'd like to eat.
(Ja bitte, Hähnchen und Pommes.)

Ask if s/he would like to go to the cinema later.
(Sollen wir später ins Kino gehen?)

Teacher's/examiner's role

Was möchtest du?

Möchtest du etwas essen?

Ja gut, ich bestelle.

Ja, gute Idee!

C Role-play 3 (Higher level)

> **TIP**
> - Check the instructions carefully: are you asked to give a certain number of details? Make sure you give the right number!

Teacher's/examiner's role

Guten Tag.

Wann haben Sie es verloren?

Wie sieht es aus? Was gibt es d'rin?

Sie sprechen gut Deutsch. Wie lange lernen Sie die Sprache?

Your card (model answer in brackets)

Du hast dein Geldbeutel verloren.
(Ich habe mein Geldbeutel verloren.)

Erkläre wann du es verloren hast.
(Ich habe es heute im Einkaufszentrum verloren, um ungefähr fünfzehn Uhr.)

Beschreibe es und sage was es d'rin gibt.
(Es ist klein und braun, aus Leder gemacht und es gibt vielleicht zwanzig Euros d'rin.)

Beantworte die Fragen, die der Beamte stellt.
(Danke, ich lerne Deutsch schon seit vier Jahren.)

Writing-exam practice

- In the writing exam, you will be asked to write a list or fill out a form, write a short message (perhaps a note to a friend or an e-mail) and write a letter including reference to the present, past and future and expressing your opinion.

- For the Higher-level paper, you will also have to do a piece of writing that shows you can use your imagination and write a description in German. This might be an article, some publicity material or something similar.

- There is some practice for each of these question types on the following pages, plus a model answer for each question.

- Try to do the questions yourself and then compare your answer to the model answer. Even if your answer is perfect, it will not be exactly the same as the model, but at least you will have an idea of whether you are doing the right thing.

A At your pen pal's house

You are visiting your pen pal for the first time. He shows you his room. Write a list of eight things you see.

Beispiel: *das Teddybär*

1 *das Teddybär*   3 _____   5 _____   7 _____
2 _____   4 _____   6 _____   8 _____

These pictures are only examples. You may include other things that are not illustrated.

Sample answer

1 das Teddybär   3 das Fenster   5 der Pullover   7 der Tisch
2 der Computer   4 die Bücher   6 die Jeans   8 die Lampe

B School

Fill in the gaps in German with a phrase or sentence suggested by the picture.

Which lesson is it?		When do you have it?
+ − × ÷	Mathematik	(Mo.) Di. Mi. Do. Fr. Sa.
		Am Montag
(scroll image)		Mo. Di. Mi. (Do.) Fr. Sa.
(flag image)		Mo. Di. Mi. Do. (Fr.) Sa.
(paint palette image)		Mo. Di. Mi. Do. Fr. (Sa.)
(globe image)		Mo. (Di.) Mi. Do. Fr. Sa.
(music notes image)		(Mo.) Di. Mi. Do. Fr. Sa.

Sample answer

Geschichte – am Donnerstag

Deutsch – am Freitag

Kunst – am Samstag

Erdkunde – am Dienstag

Musik – am Montag

C Writing an e-mail

Write an e-mail to friend in German telling them about your week at school.

Write about 40 words in complete sentences.

Write about:

- your school
- what you study
- when you have each subject
- how you travel to school.

Sample answer

Hallo Michael!

Meine Schule ist groß aber sehr nett und freundlich. Ich lerne Englisch, Mathematik, Physik, Chemie, Biologie, Kunst, Deutsch, Erdkunde und Geschichte. Mein Lieblingsfach ist Deutsch. Nächstes Jahr möchte ich nach Deutschland fahren. Heute bin ich mit dem Fahrrad in die Schule gekommen. Die Schule beginnt um neun Uhr.

Tschüs!

Stephan

Look!

- This student has written about all the things asked for in the instructions.
- He has used three tenses (past, present and future).
- The piece of writing is about 40 words long.
- It is in the format of an e-mail.
- The right form of the verb was used each time.
- The student has included opinion (favourite subject).

D About you

Schreibe ein Fax an einen neuen Brieffreund/eine neue Brieffreundin.

Erwähne die folgende Information:

- deine Familie
- dein Haus
- wo du letztes Jahr im Urlaub warst
- deine Fahrpläne für dieses Jahr
- deine Hobbys (was machst du und warum).

Schreibe 90–100 Wörter auf Deutsch

Sample answer

Liebe/r Brieffreund/in!

Ich heiße Miranda. Ich wohne mit meiner Familie — mein Vater, John, ist Mechaniker, meine Mutter, Isabel, ist Hausfrau, und meine kleine Schwester, Phoebe, ist nur zwei Jahre alt. Wir wohnen in einer Wohnung in Kingston, in Südengland.

Letztes Jahr sind wir nach Frankreich gefahren. Wir sind mit dem Auto gefahren. Das Wetter war sehr gut und wir haben viel Spaß gehabt.

Dieses Jahr werden wir nach Spanien fliegen. Wir werden zwei Wochen mit meinem Onkel verbringen! Ich freue mich sehr darauf!

Ich spiele gern Gitarre. Ich lerne seit zehn Jahren Gitarre mit meiner Mutter — sie spielt sehr gut. Ich gehe auch gern ins Theater. Das finde ich wirklich interessant.

Schreibe bald mit Information über dich!

Deine Miranda

Look!

- The student has used three tenses in this piece of writing.
- They have also expressed an opinion and said why they think something.
- It is just over 100 words long.
- They have used the proper fax format.

E Higher activity

Schreibe einen Aufsatz mit dem Titel «Unterwegs nach der Schule ist mir etwas komisches geschehen».

Erwähne die folgenden Punkte:

- Wie kommst du normalerweise zur Schule?
- Wo warst du an diesem Tag?
- Was ist geschehen? Warum?
- Was ist danach geschehen?
- Was hast du danach gemacht?
- Was denkst du darüber?

Schreibe 140–150 Wörter auf Deutsch.

Sample answer

Ich war heute unterwegs zur Schule als ich etwas interessantes gesehen habe. Ein sehr kleiner Mann saß in einem Garten vor einem Haus und spielte mit einem riesigen Hund. Der Hund war so groß, dass der Mann auf seinem Rücken reiten konnte!

Ich bin ein bißchen weiter mit meiner Freundin Elisabeth gelaufen. Wir haben darüber gesprochen. War das nicht komisch, einen solchen Mann mit einem solchen Hund zu sehen! Ich habe den Mann sehr interessant gefunden. Er schien zu einem Märchen zu gehören.

Alles auf einmal ist der Hund vor uns gesprungen. Er hat uns gesagt, dass sein Freund (der kleine Mann) eine Geschichte für uns hatte, wenn wir uns dafür eine Interesse hatten. Wir haben dem Hund gefolgt. Er ist so schnell gelaufen, dass wir ihn verloren haben. Er ist verschwunden! Wir mussten dann zur Schule laufen, so dass wir nicht verspätet waren, und wir haben ihn nie wieder gesehen.

Jeden Abend als wir von der Schule zurückkommen, fragen wir uns, ob wir ihn wieder sehen werden. Wir hoffen, dass wir das nächste Mal schneller laufen können!

Look!

- This piece of imaginative writing includes three tenses and the expression of opinion.
- There are a range of reasonably complex sentences and some unusual vocabulary – **riesig**, **verschwunden**, **gesprungen**, etc.
- This student is showing off an ability to manipulate German well.
- This is what a piece of writing of around 180 words looks like.

Topic checker

- After you've revised a topic, have a go at answering these questions.
- Put a tick if you know the answer, a cross if you don't.
- Check your answers by using the page references and looking back in the book.
- Try the questions again next time ... until you've got a column that is all ticks! Then you know you can be confident!

All about me

Self, family and friends

Can you say and spell your name and surname?	(p. 8–9)	☐	☐	☐
Can you say the German alphabet?	(p. 8–9)	☐	☐	☐
Can you say what age you are and when your birthday is?	(p. 8–9)	☐	☐	☐
Can you ask someone else questions about their name, age and birthday?	(p. 8–9)	☐	☐	☐
Can you describe what you look like?	(p. 8–9)	☐	☐	☐
Can you describe your character?	(p. 8–9)	☐	☐	☐
Can you describe all these aspects of another member of your family?	(p. 8–9)	☐	☐	☐
Can you say who the people in your family are?	(p. 8–9)	☐	☐	☐
Can you give three more pieces of information about members of your family? (job, married or single, pets?)	(p. 8–9)	☐	☐	☐

Going out

Can you say who you like to spend your time with, and why?	(p. 10–11)	☐	☐	☐
Can you say where you like to go in your spare time?	p. 10–11)	☐	☐	☐
Can you say what you can do there and why you like it?	(p. 10–11)	☐	☐	☐
Can you ask other people about what they do in their spare time, where and with whom?	(p. 10–11)	☐	☐	☐
Can you ask someone if they want to go out somewhere with you?	(p. 10–11)	☐	☐	☐
Can you arrange a time and place to meet someone?	(p. 10–11)	☐	☐	☐
Can you write an invitation to someone to go out with you?	(p. 10–11)	☐	☐	☐

All about me continued

Interests and hobbies

Can you say what sports you play?	(p. 14–15)	☐	☐	☐
Can you explain what other things you do in your free time?	(p. 14–15)	☐	☐	☐
Can you explain which pastimes you do and don't enjoy?	(p. 14–15)	☐	☐	☐
Can you say on which days you do which activities?	(p. 14–15)	☐	☐	☐

Home and local environment

Can you say where you live?	(p. 16–17)	☐	☐	☐
Can you describe your bedroom and what is in it?	(p. 16–17)	☐	☐	☐
Can you explain whether you prefer to live in the country or the town, and why?	(p. 16–17)	☐	☐	☐

Daily routine

Can you say how you get to school?	(p. 20–21)	☐	☐	☐
Can you describe how long the journey takes?	(p. 20–21)	☐	☐	☐
Can you name seven school subjects?	(p. 20–21)	☐	☐	☐
Can you say what you think of them, and why?	(p. 20–21)	☐	☐	☐
Can you say when you have certain subjects? Which day and when in the day?	(p. 20–21)	☐	☐	☐
Can you say at what time you do things?	(p. 20–21)	☐	☐	☐
Can you describe your morning routine from the moment you wake up?	(p. 20–21)	☐	☐	☐
Can you ask someone about what they do in the mornings and at what time?	(p. 20–21)	☐	☐	☐

School and future plans

Can you understand instructions in the classroom?	(p. 22–23)	☐	☐	☐
Can you describe what sort of school you go to and what the facilities are like?	(p. 22–23)	☐	☐	☐
Can you say what your favourite subject is?	(p. 22–23)	☐	☐	☐
Can you explain what you think of your teachers?	(p. 22–23)	☐	☐	☐
Can you describe what you are going to do in the summer?	(p. 22–23)	☐	☐	☐

Holiday time and travel

Travel, transport and directions

Can you name ten places in your town?	(p. 26–27)	☐	☐	☐
Can you ask for and understand directions?	(p. 26–27)	☐	☐	☐
Can you give directions using a map?	(p. 26–27)	☐	☐	☐

Tourism

Can you write a letter asking for tourist information?	(p. 28–29)	☐	☐	☐
Can you describe different activities that people might do on holiday?	(p. 28–29)	☐	☐	☐
Can you describe different holiday resorts?	(p. 28–29)	☐	☐	☐
Can you describe the weather?	(p. 28–29)	☐	☐	☐
Can you write a weather report?	(p. 28–29)	☐	☐	☐
Can you tell the time?	(p. 30–31)	☐	☐	☐

Accommodation

Can you write a letter booking holiday accommodation?	(p. 32–33)	☐	☐	☐
Can you describe facilities in a hotel and where they are?	(p. 32–33)	☐	☐	☐
Can you say if you like a hotel, and why?	(p. 32–33)	☐	☐	☐
Can you explain a problem with holiday accommodation?	(p. 32–33)	☐	☐	☐

Eating out

Can you read a menu and say what you would like to eat and drink?	(p. 34–35)	☐	☐	☐
Can you say what you like and don't like eating, and why?	(p. 34–35)	☐	☐	☐
Can you describe a meal in a restaurant and say what you ate and what happened?	(p. 34–35)	☐	☐	☐

Services

Can you recognise the names of businesses which offer a service and descriptions of what they do?	(p. 38–39)	☐	☐	☐
Can you say high numbers?	(p. 38–39)	☐	☐	☐
Can you say you want to change some money, how much and into which currency?	(p. 38–39)	☐	☐	☐

Holiday time and travel continued

Can you use the right language on the telephone in German?	(p. 38–39)	☐ ☐ ☐
Can you tell a lost property official what you have lost, where you lost it and what it looked like?	(p. 38–39)	☐ ☐ ☐

Health and safety

Can you name at least twelve parts of the body?	(p. 40–41)	☐ ☐ ☐
Can you describe an illness, where it hurts and for how long you have been ill?	(p. 40–41)	☐ ☐ ☐
Can you make an emergency call, saying where you are and what has happened?	(p. 40–41)	☐ ☐ ☐

Work and lifestyle

Home life

Can you describe what you eat in a day, what you like to eat and what you don't like, and why?	(p. 44–45)	☐ ☐ ☐
Can you say what your favourite food is?	(p. 44–45)	☐ ☐ ☐
Can you describe what jobs you do around the house, whether you like them or not, and why?	(p. 44–45)	☐ ☐ ☐

Healthy living

Can you identify healthy and unhealthy foods?	(p. 46–47)	☐ ☐ ☐
Can you compare how healthy various diets and foods are?	(p. 46–47)	☐ ☐ ☐
Can you suggest ways to have a healthy lifestyle?	(p. 46–47)	☐ ☐ ☐

Jobs and work experience

Can you say whether you get pocket money or if you have a part-time job and what you think of this situation?	(p. 50–51)	☐ ☐ ☐
Can you describe the job and what you think of it?	(p. 50–51)	☐ ☐ ☐
Can you say what you would like to become later in life?	(p. 50–51)	☐ ☐ ☐
Can you write a letter applying for a job?	(p. 50–51)	☐ ☐ ☐

Leisure

Can you say what you like to do in your spare time, and why?	(p. 52–53)	☐ ☐ ☐

Work and lifestyle continued

Can you arrange to go out with someone on the telephone?	(p. 52–53)	☐ ☐ ☐
Can you write letter describing your plans for a week's stay in a city?	(p. 52–53)	☐ ☐ ☐

At the shops

Can you make a shopping list for the supermarket?	(p. 56–57)	☐ ☐ ☐
Can you say what foods certain people can't eat, and why?	(p. 56–57)	☐ ☐ ☐
Can you ask for certain items in a shop?	(p. 56–57)	☐ ☐ ☐
Can you recognise shop names and say what you can buy in each?	(p. 56–57)	☐ ☐ ☐

At the department store

Do you know how to ask for different departments in a department store?	(p. 58–59)	☐ ☐ ☐
Can you complain about something not being quite right in a shop?	(p. 58–59)	☐ ☐ ☐
Can you say exactly what you would like to buy, including size and colour? When you see the item, can you say whether you would or wouldn't like it, and why?	(p. 58–59)	☐ ☐ ☐

It's your world

Character and relationships

Can you describe characteristics of various people and say what you think of them?	(p. 62–63)	☐ ☐ ☐
Can you describe personal problems and understand solutions offered?	(p. 62–63)	☐ ☐ ☐

The environment

Can you describe whether something is environmentally friendly or not?	(p. 64–65)	☐ ☐ ☐
Can you say what people should or must do to protect the environment?	(p. 64–65)	☐ ☐ ☐
Can you describe an event organised to improve environmental awareness?	(p. 64–65)	☐ ☐ ☐

Education

Can you compare life as a German student and life as a British student?	(p. 68–69)	☐ ☐ ☐
Can you describe problems teenagers face at school?	(p. 68–69)	☐ ☐ ☐
Can you describe your education, your school and what you like and dislike about both?	(p. 68–69)	☐ ☐ ☐

It's your world continued
Careers and future plans

Can you describe various jobs and what each involves?	(p. 70–71)	☐ ☐ ☐
Can you describe what are considered good characteristics for employees, and give your opinion about this?	(p. 70–71)	☐ ☐ ☐
Can you talk about your future plans and why you have made your choices?	(p. 70–71)	☐ ☐ ☐

Job applications

Can you make a telephone call enquiring about a job?	(p. 74–75)	☐ ☐ ☐
Can you write your CV?	(p. 74–75)	☐ ☐ ☐

Social issues

Can you write an advert for a pen pal?	(p. 76–77)	☐ ☐ ☐
Can you say what you like/dislike about the law and how it affects you?	(p. 76–77)	☐ ☐ ☐
Can you speak about when young people leave home, and why?	(p. 76–77)	☐ ☐ ☐

Grammar

Can you speak about something which has happened in the past using the perfect tense, remembering which verbs take **haben** and which take **sein**?	(p. 54–55)	☐ ☐ ☐
Can you speak about something which is planned for the future?	(p. 24–25)	☐ ☐ ☐
Can you express your opinion about something and say why you think that?	(p. 36–37)	☐ ☐ ☐

Complete the grammar

Nouns

Fill in the gaps with the word for **a** or **the**.

Masculine	_____ Mann sitzt im Bus.	A man is sitting on the bus.
	_____ Mann heißt Ulrich.	The man is called Ulrich.
Feminine	_____ Frau sitzt im Bus.	A woman is sitting on the bus.
	_____ Frau heißt Ulla.	The woman is called Ulla.
Neuter	_____ Haus liegt in der Stadt.	A house is in the city.
	_____ Haus liegt in der Stadt.	The house is in the city.

What is unusual about NOUNS in German?

Plurals

Fill in the gaps.

Gender	Masculine	Feminine	Neuter
Singular	der Mann	die Mappe	das Haus
Plural	_____ Männer	_____ Mappen	_____ Häuser

What is generally added in German to make a noun plural?

Fill in the gaps.

ein Buch   30 ....   eine Katze   3 ....

ein Kind   15 ....   ein Mann   8 ....

eine Frau   4 ....   ein Hut   2 ....

Pronouns

Would you use **du** or **Sie** when talking to these people? Write your answers in the boxes.

1 meine Deutschlehrerin

2 der Austauschschüler aus Österreich

3 unser Nachbar Herr Klose

4 Tante Ulrike aus Bonn

5 das Baby von Frau May

6 Tanjas Vater

7 unsere Katze

8 die Königin

Match the German to the English.

ich	he
du	it
er	they
sie	we
es	you (informal – friends, etc.)
man	you (more than one person)
wir	you (polite)
ihr	I
Sie	she
sie	one

Verbs 1

Present tense

Complete the grid with the correct present tense verb forms.

	schwimmen	machen	kaufen	wohnen
ich				
du				
er				
sie				
es				
man				
wir				
ihr				
Sie				
sie				

What do you notice about the endings?

Reflexive verbs

Write sentences using the correct word for **myself**, **himself**, **herself**, etc.

	infinitive	sentence
ich	sich waschen	Ich wasche mich jeden Tag.
du	sich freuen	
er/sie/es/man	sich sonnen	
wir	sich treffen	
sie	sich kämmen	

Verb as second idea

Put the two parts of these sentences together using the correct word order.

Am Montag   Ich fahre mit meiner Mutter nach London.

....

Im dritten Stock   Wir haben unsere Haushaltsabteilung.

....

Jedes Wochenende   Ich arbeite in einem Restaurant.

....

Morgen früh   Ich komme mit.

....

Um sechs Uhr   Wir treffen uns.

....

Nach den Sommerferien   Wir gehen zurück in die Schule.

....

Future tense

Insert the correct form of **werden** in the table.

ich		nach London fahren.
du		schwimmen gehen.
er		in die Stadt fahren.
sie		mit ihrer Mutter einkaufen gehen.
es		kalt sein.
man		hier treffen.
wir		diesen Film sehen.
ihr		die Arbeit nicht schwierig finden.
Sie		mit Herrn Schmidt sprechen.
sie		die Sehenswürdigkeiten besuchen.

Put these sentences into the future.

Du fährst nach Irland.   _Du wirst nach Irland fahren._ ....

Ich spiele Tischtennis.   ....

Wir singen mit dem Chor.   ....

Es regnet.   ....

Du bleibst zu Hause.   ....

Sie lernen viel.   ....

Marianne studiert Deutsch.   ....

There is another way of putting phrases into the future. What is it?

Man kann + infinitive
Put the words in the correct order to make sentences.

schwimmen kann hier man ....

man unterwegs essen kann ....

kann Italien fahren man nach ....

Montags mitmachen kann man ....

Likes, dislikes or preferences
Answer these questions (use the answers given or give your own answers).

Hast du Schokolade gern? (yes)

....

Siehst du gern fern? (no)

....

Schwimmst du gern? (prefer to play tennis)

....

Liest du gern? (yes)

....

Studierst du gern Mathematik? (yes)

....

Gehst du gern ins Kino? (no)

....

Gehst du gern ins Theater? (yes)

....

Make sentences saying whether you like these things or not and why.

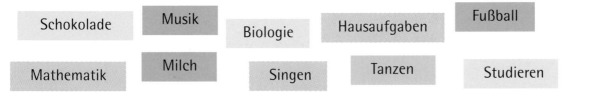

Schokolade   Musik   Biologie   Hausaufgaben   Fußball

Mathematik   Milch   Singen   Tanzen   Studieren

Schokolade gefällt mir sehr gut, weil es mir so gut schmeckt!

Telling the time
Wieviel Uhr ist es?

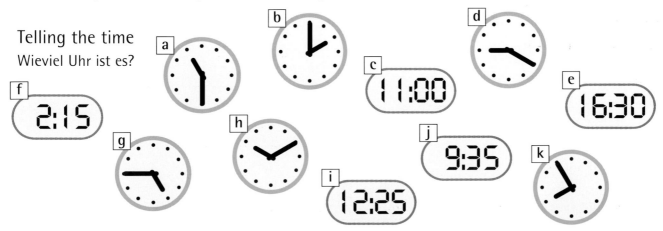

Letters

What information, apart from the date, generally goes at the top of a letter?

How many ways can you think of to start a letter?

Does this change depending on whether the letter is to a male or a female? How?

Write correctly three ways of finishing a letter. Which is suitable for what situation?

weil and other words which send the verb to the end

Make a single sentence from the two parts using **wenn**, **weil**, **dass**, **bevor** or **als**.

Ich lese dieses Buch.	Ich finde es interessant. (weil)

....

Ich war zu Hause.	Ich sah meine Katze zum ersten Mal. (als)

....

Die Familie fährt zum Strand.	Es wird schön. (wenn)

....

Wir glauben	Die Katze ist krank. (dass)

....

möchten, sollen, müssen, können, dürfen

Put these sentences in the correct order.

lange ich Wanderungen unternehmen möchte ....

ich singen darf zu nicht Hause ....

Montags machen meine ich Hausaufgaben muss ....

am schlafen Strand möchten wir ....

ich Papiertüte kaufen soll ....

kannst du am in die gehen Kirche Fuß zu Sonntag ....

später werden Ingenieurin möchte ich ....

Verbs 2

Separable verbs

Make sentences.

aufstehen (ich – um acht Uhr)   _Ich stehe um acht Uhr auf._

ankommen (der Zug – um sieben Uhr)   ....

abspülen (meine Schwester – jeden Tag) ....

abtrocknen (ich – abends)   ....

aufstehen (meine Freundin – um sechs Uhr) ....

ankommen (wir – in London um achtzehn Uhr) ....

abspülen (mein Bruder – zu Hause)   ....

abtrocknen (Eloise – Montags)   ....

Some irregular verbs

Complete the grid.

sein	Ich _____zwanzig Jahre alt.	I am twenty years old.
sein	Er _____ zu jung.	He is too young.
essen	Sie _____ kein Fleisch.	She doesn't eat meat.
haben	Er _____ eine Katze.	He has a cat.
fahren	Man _____ mit dem Auto.	We go by bus.
lesen	Er _____ zu viel.	He reads too much.
nehmen	Sandra_____die Tasse.	Sandra takes the cup.
sehen	Georg_____ fern.	Georg watches TV.
schlafen	Sie _____bis zwölf Uhr.	She sleeps until midday.
helfen	_____du zu Hause?	Do you help at home?

Perfect tense

Complete the grid.

ich	habe
du	
er/sie/es/man	
wir/Sie/sie	
ihr	

Complete the grid.

infinitive	English	past participle	sentence
kaufen	to buy	gekauft	Ich habe eine Katze gekauft
machen			
spielen			
lernen			
wohnen			
sagen			
fragen			
hören			

What happens to the past participle in a sentence?

Irregular past participles

Complete the grid.

infinitive	English	past participle	sentence
lesen	to read	gelesen	Ich habe dieses Buch gelesen.
sehen			
singen			
essen			
bringen			
helfen			
werfen			

Some exceptions

How do these verbs change into past participles?

reservieren Ich habe ein Zimmer reserviert.

telefonieren

reparieren

besuchen

bedanken

erzählen

erleben

verkaufen

vermeiden

What do you notice about these past participles?

Separable verbs in the past

Make these verbs into past participles.

infinitive	past participle	English
aufstehen		
anfangen		
ankommen		
einschalten		
aufräumen		

Verbs which take sein (not haben)

infinitive	English	sentence
fahren	to travel	Ich bin nach Luxemburg gefahren.
fliegen		
kommen		
gehen		
laufen		
reiten		
schwimmen		
werden		
verschwinden		
passieren		
bleiben		
sterben		

What do you notice about these verbs?

Imperfect tense
Match the infinitive to the correct imperfect form.

sein	wir machten
machen	ich war
haben	er könnte
können	du hattest
sollen	Sie wollte
wollen	ich sollte

Complete the following grid for the imperfect tense.

	haben	sein
ich	hatte	war
du		
er/sie/es/man		
wir/Sie/sie		

When do you use the imperfect tense?

Question words

Match the following question words with their correct meaning, then cover the first column and write the German question words again.

German	Wrong English	Right English	Right German
wie	what		
was	when		
wo	why		
warum	how		
wann	where		
wer	how many		
wieviel	who		

Accusative (direct object) case

Complete the grids.

nominative (subject)	der	die	das	die
accusative				

	masculine	feminine	neuter	plural
nominative (subject)	ein	eine	ein	keine
accusative				

Masculine object (der Mann)

Ich sehe _____ Mann. (the)

Ich sehe _____ Mann. (a)

Feminine object

Ich habe _____ Flasche. (the)

Ich habe _____ Flasche. (a)

Neuter object

Ich kaufe _____ Haus. (the)

Ich kaufe _____ Haus. (a)

Only one of the genders changes at all in the accusative case. Which one is it?

Complete the grid with the correct form after **es gibt**.

	a/the	turns into	a/the
masculine	ein/der Bahnhof	→	Es gibt _____ /_____ Bahnhof.
feminine	eine/die Kirche	→	Es gibt _____ /_____ Kirche.
neuter	ein/das Stadion	→	Es gibt _____ /_____ Stadion.
plural	Autos	→	Es gibt Autos.

Adjective agreement – accusative (direct object) case

Write some example sentences.

	masc.	fem.	neut.	plural
accusative/ direct object	einen	eine	ein	keine
adjective ending	-en	-e	-es	-e
example sentence				

Dative (indirect object) case

Complete the grids.

nominative (subject)	der	die	das	die
accusative	den	die	das	die
dative				

	masculine	feminine	neuter	plural
nominative (subject)	ein	eine	ein	keine
accusative	einen	eine	ein	keine
dative				

Prepositions

Accusative

Complete the grid.

English	German	sentence
until		
through		
for		
without		

Dative

Complete the grid.

English	German	sentence
opposite		
with		
out of		
at the home of		
after		
since		
to		
from		

Accusative or dative

German	English with movement (acc)	English without movement (dat)	sentence
auf	onto	on	Ich stelle die Kassette auf *den* Tisch. Die Kassette ist auf *dem* Tisch.
in	into	inside	Du gehst in _____ Stadt. (die) Du bist in _____ Stadt. (die)
neben	by the side of	next to	Er geht neben_____Haus. (das) Er sitzt neben _____ Haus. (das)
über	over the top of	above	Sie fliegt über_____ Geschäft. (das) Sie wohnt über _____ Geschäft. (das)
unter	underneath	below	Man läuft unter_____ Baum. (der) Man sitzt unter_____ Baum. (der)
vor	in front of	in front of	Ich schwimme vor _____Haus. (das) Ich sitze vor _____ Haus. (das)

Complete the following sentences

1 Ich bleibe _____ . (I'm staying at home.)

2 Ich fahre _____ . (I'm travelling by bus.)

3 Ich gehe _____ . (I'm walking.)

4 Wie sagt man das _____? (How do you say that in German?)

5 Wir wohnen _____ . (We live in the country.)

6 _____ Weihnachten (at Christmas)

7 Er fährt _____ . (He's going abroad.)

8 _____ Jahren (three years ago)

Possessives

Complete the grid.

my	mein
your	
his	
her	
our	
their	

How do these possessives change in the accusative?

Pronouns

How do these pronouns change in the accusative and the dative?

nominative(subject)	accusative (object)	dative
ich	mich	mir
du		
er		
sie		
es		
wir		
ihr		
Sie		
sie		

Quick quiz

1 What is **in dem** shortened to?
2 What is **zu dem** shortened to?
3 What is **zu der** shortened to?
4 What is the rule about 'half past' in German?
5 What word do you use to mean <u>at</u> a time (e.g. at 12 o'clock)?
6 What word do you use to mean <u>on</u> a day (e.g. on Sunday)?
7 If something happens regularly (e.g. every Sunday) how do you say that?
8 What word do you use to mean <u>in</u> a month or season (e.g. in January/in the summer)?
9 How do you say that something happens on a certain date?
10 How do you write the date at the top of a letter?
11 How do you say <u>from</u> a certain date <u>until</u> another?

Self, family and friends

C

1   1 d   2 e   3 a   4 c   5 b

Going out

B

1   a auf dem Land   b ins Freibad   c ins Kino

Interests and hobbies

A

1   a Tennis   c Tanzen   e Tischtennis
    b Fußball   d Gitarre   f Computer

B

1   a 4   b 2   c 3   d 1   e 5

D

1   a N   b N   c F   d F   e F

Home and local environment

A

1   a Buch – 2   c Teddybär – 3   e Computer – 4
    b Kleider – 5   d Fernseher – 1

B

1   in der Stadt – a, b   auf dem Land – c, d
2   Vorteile – a, b, d   Nachteile – c

C

1   Schlafzimmer, Küche, Badezimmer, Dachgeschoss, Keller, Garten

Daily routine

A

1   1 b, g   2 c, h   3 a, e   4 d, f

B

1

1. Stunde	2. Stunde	3. Stunde	4. Stunde	5. Stunde
Mathe	Englisch	Geschichte	Biologie	Musik
Deutsch	Physik	Mathe	Englisch	Theater
Englisch	Deutsch	Informatik	Chemie	Mathe
Biologie	Mathe	Deutsch	Theater	Englisch
Deutsch	Erdkunde	Kunst	Englisch	Chemie

C

2   a 6.50   b 7.15   c 15 Minuten   d 12.00–12.45   e 14.00

School and future plans

A

1   a Beantworte die Fragen.   d Gib Information über …
    b Mache einen Dialog.   e Finde die passenden Bilder.
    c Schreibe die Details auf.

2   a Answer the questions.   d Give information about …
    b Create a dialogue.   e Find the correct pictures.
    c Write the details down.

B

2   1 c   2 b   3 d   4 e   5 a

Travel, transport and directions

A

1   a die Post   d das Krankenhaus
    b die Bank   e das Geschäft
    c die Garage   f die Kirche

Tourism

C

1   Ulrich – 1   Markus – 4   Gerthrud – 3

Accommodation

A

1   a Susanna   d eine frankierte Postkarte
    b sechs (6)   e 27. August
    c Bad Marienberg, Freiburg

C

1   a 4   b 3   c 1   d 2

Eating out

A

2   a falsch   b falsch   c richtig   d falsch

B

1   5, 3, 1, 6, 4, 2, 7

Services

A

1   a die Post   d die Apotheke
    b das Fundbüro   e die Telefonzelle
    c der Geldautomat   f der Fahrradverleih

2   a die Telefonzelle   c der Geldautomat
    b das Fundbüro   d der Fahrradverleih

B

1   a Hier spricht Johann.   f Kann ich bitte eine
    b Hallo.   Nachricht hinterlassen?
    c Auf Wiederhören.   g Leider ist er im Moment
    d Ein Moment, bitte.   nicht da.
    e Wer spricht, bitte?   h Ich rufe später an.

C

1   a zwanzig   e fünfzig
    b hundert   f fünfundsiebzig
    c zehn   g zweihundertfünfzig
    d dreißig

Practice

1   1 c   2 b   3 d   4 e   5 a

2   a Ich habe meine   c Irgendwo im Museum.
      Armbanduhr verloren.   d Sie hat einen Band aus Leder.
    b Vor drei Stunden.   e Braun.

Health and safety

B

1   1 b   2 a   3 d   4 c

Home life

A

2 Marko – Ich muss abwaschen und abtrocknen.
Matthias – Ich muss einmal in der Woche die Mülltonne leeren.
Sylvia – Ich muss mein Zimmer aufräumen und mein Bett machen.

B

1 Silke hat den Tisch gedeckt, die Mülltonne geleert, ihr Bett gemacht, ihren Hund gefüttert und hat abgetrocknet.
Mehmet hat abgespült, hat sein Zimmer aufgeräumt, und hat staubgesaugt. Er hat das Auto seines Vaters geputzt.
Marko hat abgespült und abgetrocknet.
Matthias hat die Mülltonne geleert.
Sylvia hat ihr Zimmer aufgeräumt und ihr Bett gemacht.

C

2 Cornflakes, Müsli, Orangensaft, Obst, Suppe, Hähnchen, Pommes, Pizza, Currywurst, belegten Brötchen, Spaghetti Bolognese, chinesisches Stir Fry, Steak, Tomatensuppe mit Toast, Spiegeleier, Speck, Bohnen in Tomatensoße, Würstchen

Healthy living

C

1 a Friedrich   b Max   c Rin

Jobs and work experience

B

1 a Koch   c Briefträger   e Polizist
   b Mechaniker   d Ingenieur   f Kellner

Leisure

A

1 a 2   b 3   c 1

At the shops

B

1 Disketten, Gläser
2 Marko – c Fleischwurst   Sylvia – d Kopfsalat
  Lukas – f Fruchtjoghurt   Micki   – a Konfitüre

C

1 a eine Flasche Limonade   d ein Tafel Schokolade
   b zweihundert Gramm Schinken e sechs Brötchen
   c ein Stück Käse   f eine Dose Karotten

Practice

2 a 2   b 1   c 3

At the department store

A

1 1 d   2 e   3 a   4 b   5 c
2 a Im dritten Stock.   c Im Erdgeschoss.
   b Im ersten Stock.   d Im Untergeschoss.

B

1 1 b   2 c   3 d   4 a

C

1 1 c   2 a   3 b

Character and relationships

B

1 Lucia ist interessant, lebendig, lustig, und kann ein bisschen diktatorisch sein.
Max ist intelligent, fleißig, optimistisch und manchmal launisch.

C

1 a 2   b 1   c 1   d 2

The environment

A

1 c ✓   d ✗   e ✓   f ✓

B

1 b Man soll nie mit dem Auto fahren, man muss immer Fahrrad fahren oder zu Fuß gehen.
   c Man soll nie normales Reinigungsmittel kaufen, man muss immer phosphatfreies Reinigungsmittel kaufen.
   d Man soll keine Glasflaschen wegwerfen, man muss alle Flaschen recyceln.
   e Man soll kein Papier in den Mülleimer werfen, man muss alles Papier in die grüne Tonne werfen.
   f Mann soll jede Woche keine neue Plastiktüte nehmen, man muss Taschen aus Stoff oder Altpapier benutzen.

Education

A

1 a Deutschland   c Großbritannien   e Deutschland
   b Deutschland   d Großbritannien

Careers and future plans

B

1 a Zuverlässigkeit   c Ehrlichkeit
   b Freundlichkeit   d ein niedriger Prozentsatz

C

1 1 d   2 c   3 e   4 a   5 b

Job applications

A

1

NAME:	Scherer, Elisabeth
ALTER:	17
GEBURTSDATUM:	9. Oktober 1981
ADRESSE:	Feigenberg 26, 6729 Hatzenbühl
TELEFONNUMMER:	07275 2425
SCHULBILDUNG:	1987–1992 Gundschule in Jockrim
	1992–2000 Goethe-Gymnasium, Wörth
	seit 2000 – Universität Trier
HOBBYS:	Tiere, Umweltschutz, Lesen, Schwimmen

C

2 a Marla Friedhof
   b 29. August 1985
   c Dresden
   d 2 (ein Bruder und eine Schwester)
   e Kaiserdamm 45, 8350 München
   f Sie besuchte die Grundschule in der Stadtmitte Dresden.

g Jetzt macht sie ihr Abitur.

h Sie möchte später Informatikerin werden.

Social issues

C

1 a richtig   b falsch   c falsch   d richtig

Answers to 'Listening-exam practice'

A

3 Deutsch, Englisch, Französisch, Mathe, Geschichte

4 Biologie, Kunst, Latein, Musik, Politik, Sport, Theater

B

3 Austen – Mathe; Irina – Mathe und Physik; Simon – Sport und Politik; Ivanka – Mathe; Svenja – Mathe und Englisch; Natalie – Chemie und Erdkunde; Stefan – Deutsch, Englisch, Latein, Physik, Biologie, Religion, Kunst, Musik

C

3 halb acht (f), acht Uhr (c), neun Uhr (g), fünf Uhr (a), sieben Uhr (h), drei Uhr (b)

D

2 Constance's room – das Bett, die Kleidung, Poster, Teddybären; Wohnzimmer – Andenken aus Afrika, das Bild, der Bücherschrank, der Fernseher, die Stereoanlage

E

1 gesund – Gemüse, Nudeln, Obst, Sport, Vitamine; nicht gesund – Bonbons, Drogen, Fleisch, Hamburger, Pommes frites, Rauchen, Schokolade, Süßigkeiten

F

3 Frau – Kartoffelsalat, Würstchen; Mann – Pommes frites, Wiener Schnitzel, gemischter Salat

4 Woman drinks ein Bier.

G

2 a Thomas, b Marko, c Esther, d Miriam, e Jessica

3 einen Bruder – Ivanka, Christopher, Katrin, Irina, Nada, Stefan, Michael; eine Schwester – Katrin, Ulrike; keine Geschwister – Cecilia, Sabine

4 Constances Bruder: Name: Michael; Alter: 21; Haare: braun; Augen: braun; Größe: 2 Meter

Christophers Bruder: Alter: 11; Haare: blond; Augen: blau; Er ist: manchmal ganz nett; manchmal ziemlich nervig

Irinas Bruder: Alter: 19; Haare: blond; Er ist: groß und hübsch

H

2 Im Winter – Curling, Eisstockschießen, Rodeln, Schlittschuhlaufen, Schwimmen, Skilaufen; Im Sommer – Bergsteigen, Fallschirmspringen, Kajak fahren, Klettern, Mountainbike fahren, Wandern

I

1 a bei McDonald's b   um eins

2 a in die Kantine b   um zwölf

J

2 1c, 2a, 3d, 4b

K

2 1 zu Fuß; 2 mit der Bahn; 3 mit dem Bus und der Bahn; 4 mit dem Fahrrad; 5 mit dem Auto

L

2 1c, 2b, 3a

M

2 a eine Fahrkarte nach Düsseldorf, b für heute, c hin und zurück, d kostet 85,20 DM

N

2 b, d, e, g, h

O

1 f, c, e, d, b, a

3 1b, 2a, 3b, 4a, 5b

P

2 1a, 2b, 3a, 4a, 5b, 6a

Q

2 Amerika, Australien und Neuseeland, der Dschungel, Hawaii, Kanada, die Karibik, eine Weltreise, die Wüste

R

2 1b, 2a, 3a, 4b, 5b, 6a

Answers to 'Complete the grammar'

Nouns

ein, der, eine, die, ein, das

Nouns ALWAYS have a capital letter.

Plurals

die, die, die

Mostly nouns add –e or –en but there are many exceptions where umlauts and other endings might be used. Like gender (**der, die, das**) the best way to get to know these is to learn them!

Bücher, Kinder, Frauen, Katzen, Männer, Hüte

Pronouns

1 Sie	3 Sie	5 du	7 du
2 du	4 du	6 Sie	8 Sie

ich – I

du – you (informal – friends etc.)

er – he

sie – she

es – it

man – one

wir – we

ihr – you (more than one person)

Sie – you (polite)

sie – they

Verbs 1

Present tense

ich schwimme, du schwimmst, er/sie/es/man schwimmt, wir/Sie/sie schwimmen, ihr schwimmt; ich mache, du machst, er/sie/es/man macht, wir/Sie/sie machen, ihr macht; ich kaufe, du kaufst, er/sie/es/man kauft, wir/Sie/sie kaufen, ihr kauft; ich wohne, du wohnst, er/sie/es/man wohnt, wir/Sie/sie wohnen, ihr wohnt.

The endings for **er**, **sie**, **es** and **man** are the same, the endings for **wir**, **Sie** and **sie** are the same. That makes fewer to learn!

Reflexive verbs

Du freust dich auf die Party; Er sonnt sich im Garten; Wir treffen uns um vier Uhr; Sie kämmen sich jetzt.

Verb as second idea

Am Montag fahre ich mit meiner Mutter nach London.
Im dritten Stock haben wir unsere Haushaltsabteilung.
Jedes Wochenende arbeite ich in einem Restaurant.
Morgen früh komme ich mit.
Um sechs Uhr treffen wir uns.
Nach den Sommerferien gehen wir zurück in die Schule.

Future tense

ich werde, du wirst, er/sie/es/man wird, wir/Sie/sie werden, ihr werdet

Ich werde Tischtennis spielen.
Wir werden mit dem Chor singen.
Es wird regnen.
Du wirst zu Hause bleiben.
Sie werden viel lernen.
Marianne wird Deutsch studieren.

Use a phrase in the future like **nächste Woche/in zwei Jahren** and the present tense.

Man kann + infinitive

Man kann hier schwimmen.
Man kann unterwegs essen.
Man kann nach Italien fahren.
Man kann Montags mitmachen.

Telling the time

a halb zwölf **b** vierzehn Uhr **c** elf Uhr **d** einundzwanzig Uhr zwanzig **e** sechzehn Uhr dreißig **f** Viertel nach zwei **g** Viertel vor fünf **h** zehn nach zehn **i** fünfundzwanzig nach zwölf **j** fünfundzwanzig vor zehn **k** fünf vor acht

Letters

town

Liebe (female)/Lieber (male) ...; Sehr geehrte Frau ... (female)/Sehr geehrter Herr ... (male)

viele Grüße (informal); Dein/Deine (informal); Hochachtungsvoll (formal)

weil and other words which send the verb to the end

Ich lese dieses Buch weil ich es interessant finde.

Ich war zu Hause als ich meine Katze zum ersten Mal sah.
Die Familie fährt zum Strand wenn es schön wird.
Wir glauben dass die Katze krank ist.

möchten, sollen, müssen, können, dürfen

Ich möchte lange Wanderungen unternehmen.
Zu Hause darf ich nicht singen.
Montags muss ich meine Hausaufgaben machen.
Wir möchten am Strand schlafen.
Ich soll Papiertüte kaufen.
Am Sonntag kannst du zu Fuß in die Kirche gehen.
Ich möchte später Ingenieurin werden.

Verbs 2

Separable verbs

Der Zug kommt um sieben Uhr an.
Meine Schwester spült jeden Tag ab.
Ich trockne abends ab.
Meine Freundin steht um sechs Uhr auf.
Wir kommen um achtzehn Uhr in London an.
Mein Bruder spült zu Hause ab.
Montags trocknet Eloise ab.

Some irregular verbs

bin, ist, isst, hat, fährt, liest, nimmt, sieht, schläft, hilfst

Perfect tense

du hast, er/sie/es/man hat, wir/Sie/sie haben, ihr habt
to do or to make, gemacht, Ich habe meine Hausaufgaben gemacht.
to play, gespielt, Wir haben Karten gespielt.
to learn, gelernt, Er hat Italienisch gelernt.
to live, gewohnt, Sie haben im Ausland gewohnt.
to say, gesagt, Man hat das immer gesagt.
to ask, gefragt, Wir haben schon gefragt.
to hear, gehört, Hast du etwas gehört?

The past participle goes to the end.

Irregular past participles

to see, gesehen, Ich habe meinen Lehrer gesehen.
to sing, gesungen, Sie hat ein schönes Lied gesungen.
to eat, gegessen, Er hat drei Äpfel gegessen.
to bring, gebracht, Mutti hat mich zur Schule gebracht.
to help, geholfen, Ich habe zu Hause viel geholfen.
to throw, geworfen, Sie hat den Ball geworfen.

Some exceptions

telefoniert   besucht   erzählt   verkauft
repariert   bedankt   erlebt   vermeidet

The past participle does not begin with **ge-**. This is generally the case with verbs which begin with **ver-**, **er-** or **be-** or that end in **-ieren**.

Separable verbs in the past

aufgestanden – got up
angefangen – began
angekommen – arrived

eingeschaltet – switched on
aufgeräumt – cleared up

Verbs which take sein (not haben)

to fly, Wir sind nach Spanien geflogen.
to come, Er ist zur Schule gekommen.
to go (on foot), Wir sind in die Stadt gegangen.
to run, Sie ist sehr schnell gelaufen.
to ride, Ich bin auf dem Lande geritten.
to swim, Wir sind im See geschwommen.
to become, Er ist später Polizist geworden.
to disappear, Mein Buch ist verschwunden.
to happen, Was ist passiert?
to stay, Du bist gestern zu Hause geblieben.
to die, Meine Oma ist letztes Jahr gestorben.

The verbs which take **sein** as past participles are almost all verbs of movement. The last five listed are the main exceptions.

Imperfect tense

sein – ich war, machen – wir machten, haben – du hattest, können – er könnte, sollen – ich sollte, wollen – Sie wollte

du hattest, du warst; er/sie/es/man hatte, er/sie/es/man war; wir/Sie/sie hatten, wir/Sie/sie waren

You use the imperfect tense to speak about something which happened in the past or which used to happen. It is most common in its written form, so it's important to be able to recognise it and know what it means.

Question words

wie – how, was – what, wo – where, warum – why, wann – when, wer – who, wieviel – how many

Accusative (direct object) case

| den | die | das | die |
| einen | eine | ein | keine |

den, einen
die, eine
das, ein

The masculine is the only gender to change in the accusative.

einen, den
eine, die
ein, das

Adjective agreement – accusative (direct object) case

Er sieht einen alten Mann.
Er sieht eine schöne Frau.
Er sieht ein kleines Kind.
Er sieht keine junge Leute.

Dative (indirect object) case

dem, der, dem, den
einem, einer, einem, keinen

Prepositions

Accusative

bis, Der Film läuft bis nächste Woche.
durch Sie fährt schnell durch die Stadt.
für, Ich habe ein Geschenk für dich.
ohne, Du kannst nicht ohne mich gehen.

Dative

gegenüber, Der Marktplatz ist gegenüber dem Dom.
mit, Kommst du mit mir ins Kino?
aus, Wann ist er aus dem Haus gegangen?
bei, Ich möchte bei Ihnen drei Nächte bleiben.
nach, Nach der Schule spielen wir Fußball.
seit, Seit den Ferien langweile ich mich.
zu, Ich komme zu dir am Montag.
von, Das habe ich von meinem Lehrer gelernt.

Accusative or dative

die, der
das, dem
das, dem
den, dem
das, dem

zu Hause, mit dem Bus, zu Fuß, auf deutsch, auf dem Land, zu, ins Ausland, vor drei.

Possessives

dein, sein, ihr, unser, ihr

In the accusative, the possessives change in the same way as ein.

Pronouns

dich, dir; ihn, ihm; sie, ihr; es, ihm; uns, uns; euch, euch; Sie, Ihnen; sie, ihnen

Quick quiz

1 im
2 zum
3 zur
4 You say 'half to' the next hour (e.g. 9.30 = halb zehn).
5 um
6 am Sonntag/am Dienstag
7 Add an s and make the first letter of the day small (e.g. sonntags)
8 im Januar/im Sommer
9 Use am and add (s)ten to the number (except ersten, dritten, siebten): am elften Dezember.
10 den 5. April. You should also write the town name (e.g. London, den 17. Juli).
11 Vom ersten bis zum dritten Dezember.

Last-minute learner

- The next four pages give you the key vocabulary across the whole subject in the smallest possible space.
- You can use these pages as a final check.
- You can also use them as you revise as a way to check your learning.
- You can cut them out for quick and easy reference.

Numbers

				dreiundzwanzig	23	achtzig	80
				vierundzwanzig	24	neunzig	90
eins	1	zwölf	12	fünfundzwanzig	25	hundert	100
zwei	2	dreizehn	13	sechsundzwanzig	26	einhunderteins	101
drei	3	vierzehn	14	siebenundzwanzig	27	zweihundert	200
vier	4	fünfzehn	15	achtundzwanzig	28	dreihundert	300
fünf	5	sechzehn	16	neunundzwanzig	29	vierhundert	400
sechs	6	siebzehn	17	dreißig	30	fünfhundert	500
sieben	7	achtzehn	18	einunddreißig	31	sechshundert	600
acht	8	neunzehn	19	vierzig	40	siebenhundert	700
neun	9	zwanzig	20	fünfzig	50	achthundert	800
zehn	10	einundzwanzig	21	sechzig	60	neunhundert	900
elf	11	zweiundzwanzig	22	siebzig	70	tausend	1000

Days of the week

Montag Dienstag Mittwoch Donnerstag Freitag
Samstag/Sonnabend Sonntag das Wochenende

Months of the year

Januar Februar März April Mai Juni Juli August
September Oktober November Dezember

Section 1: All about me (p. 8–25)

Me and my family

Ich heiße mit Vornamen (Max) und mit Familiennamen (Schmidt). Man schreibt das (M-A-X S-C-H-M-I-D-T). Ich bin (sechzehn) Jahre alt. Ich habe am (neunzehnten Januar) Geburtstag. Ich bin (mittelgroß), meine Haare sind (dunkelbraun) und meine Augen sind (blau). Ich bin (sehr/ganz/ziemlich fleißig)!
Kannst du deine Familie beschreiben? Meine Schwester heißt (Elisabeth) und sie ist (zehn) Jahre alt. Ich habe auch einen Bruder, (Lukas). Er ist (vier) Jahre alt. Meine Mutter, (Sandra), arbeitet (in einem Büro) und mein Vater ist (Ingenieur).

Hobbies

Was machst du in deiner Freizeit? Ich verbringe gern Zeit mit (meiner Stiefschwester), weil sie (lustig) ist. Wir gehen (samstagabends) (in die Disko). Wir (tanzen bis spät in die Nacht). Wir gehen heute abend (ins Kino). Wir treffen uns um (acht) Uhr (vor der Kirche). Kommst du mit? (Montags) gehe ich (schwimmen). Ich (lese) auch sehr gern und (spiele gern Tennis).

Home

Wie ist dein Zimmer, dein Haus und deine Gegend? Mein Zimmer ist (ziemlich groß/klein). Es gibt (ein Bett) (in einer Ecke). Mein (Schreibtisch) steht (neben dem Fenster). (Auf der Wand) habe ich (viele Posters) und (mein Teddybär) liegt (auf meinem Bett). Mein Haus ist (nicht sehr) groß. Es hat (drei) Schlafzimmer, ein Wohnzimmer, (ein) Badezimmer, eine Küche und einen großen Garten. Wir wohnen (in die Stadt/auf dem Land). Das (gefällt mir/gefällt mir nicht), weil (es da so viel los ist/es immer etwas zu tun gibt/die Luft immer so schmutzig ist/es nichts zu tun gibt/die Landschaft so schön ist).

Daily routine

Ich stehe um (sieben Uhr) auf. Ich frühstücke um (halb acht). Ich fahre (mit dem Schulbus/zu Fuß/mit dem Auto) nach der Schule. Wir fahren um (Viertel vor acht) ab. Die Fahrt dauert (zehn Minuten). Die Schule beginnt um (Viertel nach acht). Die Schule ist um (Viertel vor drei) aus. Ich fahre dann nach Hause. Nachmittags mache ich meine Hausaufgaben. Ich esse (um sechs Uhr) mit der Familie, dann (sehe ich fern) mit (meinem Bruder). Manchmal (spielen wir abends auch Karten). Um (halb zehn) gehe ich ins Bett.

School

In der Schule lernen wir (Mathematik, Englisch, Deutsch). Mein Lieblingsfach ist (Deutsch). (Man kann so viel mit Sprachen machen). Die Schule gefällt mir (nicht). Ich lerne (sehr/nicht) gern. Meine Schule ist (ganz groß/ klein) mit (150) Schülern. Es gibt (8) Lehrer. Sie sind (meistens sehr nett/manchmal zu streng).
Im Sommer, nach den Prüfungen, habe ich vor (nach Italien/Deutschland/Amerika) zu fahren. Da möchte ich (auf dem Strand schlafen/viel Sport treiben/viel lesen/arbeiten).
Ich besuche (das Gymnasium Trier) Die Schule ist ganz (klein/groß) mit ungefähr (1500) Schüler. In der Schule gibt es (einen Schulhof/eine Bibliothek/ein Schwimmbad/(45) Klassenzimmer/eine Sporthalle). Nach der Schule habe ich vor, (nach Israel/Amerika/Thailand zu fahren/für meinen Eltern zu arbeiten/noch zwei Jahren zu studieren). Die Schule gefällt mir (besonders gut/überhaupt nicht).

Around town

Wie ist der Markt/die Post/die Kirche in deiner Stadt? Er/sie/es ist (neu/alt/modern/altmodisch/hübsch/hässlich). Wie komme ich am besten zum Rathaus? Nimm (die erste Straße rechts), geh (über die Brücke), geh (geradeaus) und da ist es, (gegenüber der Kirche).

Holiday information

Ich rufe aus (England) an. Ich werde (Berlin/Frankfurt/Linz) im Sommer besuchen. Können Sie mir bitte (eine Broschüre über die Sehenswürdigkeiten/einen Stadplan/einen Fahrplan) zusenden? Meine Adresse ist (...). Man schreibt das (...). Im Urlaub (laufe ich gern Ski/zelte ich gern/segle ich gern). Es macht mir Spaß (aktiv zu sein/auf die Küste mich zu entspannen/ausländisches Essen zu genießen/über Architektur und Geschichte zu lernen).

Weather

Wie ist das Wetter? Das Wetter ist für's Urlaub sehr wichtig. Für mich muss es (sonnig/schön/windig/kalt/wirklich heiß) sein. Heute gibt es (Regen/ein Gewitter/Nebel/Temperaturen unter null Grad). Das finde ich (toll/überhaupt nicht schön)!

Hotels

Im (Sommer/Winter/Frühling) habe ich vor nach (Bern/Wien/Recklinghausen) zu fahren. Ich möchte (eine Nacht/zwei/zehn/zwanzig Nächte) bei Ihnen übernachten. Ich möchte ein Zimmer (mit Dusche) vom (15. Juli) bis zum (19. Juli) reservieren. Gibt es (ein Fitnesszimmer/ein Schwimmbad/eine Garage/ein Restaurant) im Hotel?
Mein Zimmer ist (zu warm/kalt). (Die Dusche/das Bad/das Licht) funktioniert nicht. Das Essen schmeckt (sehr gut/lecker/nicht besonders gut).

Restaurants

Wir essen heute abend in einem (französichen/japanischen/italienischen) (Restaurant/Schnellimbiss/Café). Können wir bitte die Speisekarte sehen? Ich nehme (ein Glas Rotwein/Weißwein/Bier/Orangensaft). Ich esse (Schnitzel/Steak/Currywurst/Fisch/Hähnchen) mit (Pommes/Kartoffelsalat/Nudeln/Salat). Die Rechnung bitte. Danke. Auf Wiedersehen. Ich esse sehr gern (Steak), das schmeckt mir sehr gut. Ich esse überhaupt nicht gern (Fisch), das schmeckt mir einfach nicht. Ich (liebe/esse nicht gern) (salziges/würziges/saueres/süßes) Essen. Letzte Woche habe ich (mit meiner Mutter) in (einem Restaurant) gegessen. Wir haben (Fisch) bestellt mit (Pommes und Salat). Ich habe auch (eine Limonade) und (meine Mutter) hat (ein kleines Glas Weißwein) getrunken. Das war (sehr schön). Abends mit (meiner Mutter) machen immer sehr viel Spaß!

Bank

Ich möchte Geld wechseln. Guten Tag, ich möchte (zwanzig Pfund) in (Euros) wechseln.

Telephone

Ich möchte zu Hause anrufen. Guten Tag, (Schmidt). Hier spricht (Frau Bauer). Kann ich bitte mit (Elisabeth Monch) sprechen? Sie ist leider im Moment nicht da. Kann ich bitte eine Nachricht lassen? Ich rufe später an.

Reporting a loss

Wie kann ich Ihnen helfen? Ich habe (meine Jacke) verloren. Wo haben Sie (sie) verloren? Ich war (am Bahnhof). Wie sieht (die Jacke) aus? Sie ist (braun und schwarz gestreift mit «Berlin» auf den Rücken geschrieben). Wann haben Sie (die Jacke) verloren? (Heute Nachmittag), zwischen (drei) und (vier) Uhr.

Health and safety

(Mein Kopf/mein Fuß/mein Hals) tut weh. Ich habe (Bauchschmerzen/Zahnschmerzen/Rückenschmerzen). Du sollst (den Zahnarzt/den Arzt/die Apotheke) anrufen. Ich habe (eine Panne/einen Unfall gehabt). Mein Auto funktioniert nicht mehr. Ich bin (auf der Autobahn/Straße) zwischen (Metzdorf) und (Hatzenbühl).

Section 3: Work and lifestyle (p. 44–61)

Food

Ich esse (gern/lieber/Am liebsten esse ich)
(Würstchen/Wiener
Schnitzel/Brot/Käse/Speck/Spiegeleier/Pommes/Bohnen/G
urkensalat/Kuchen/Schokolade).

Helping at home

Zu Hause muss ich (einkaufen
gehen/abspülen/aufräumen/abtrocknen/Staub
saugen/den Tisch decken). Ich bekomme Taschengeld
dafür, etwa (5) Euros pro Woche.

Healthy living

(Thunfisch/Salat/Obst) ist sehr gesund. (Kuchen/
Schokoladeneis) ist ungesund. (Gemüse/Fisch) wäre
gesünder als (Pommes/Hamburger). Ich möchte
(abnehmen/Topfit werden/gesünder werden).

Jobs

(Ich arbeite in einem Geschäft/beim Friseur/ich putze
Autos). Ich bekomme dafür (15) Euros pro Woche. Ich
gebe mein Geld für (CDs/Zeitschriften/Schminken/
Bücher/Geschenke) aus.

Ich möchte später Mechaniker(in)/Briefträger(in)/
Polizist(in)/Arzt/Ärztin) werden. Ich interessiere mich für
diese Stelle, weil (ich mich sehr gut mit Leuten
verstehe/ich gut mit Computern umgehen kann/ich eine
geborene Führungspersönlichkeit bin/ich sehr organisiert
bin).
Die folgenden Eigenschaften sind für Personalchefs
wichtig: Zuverlässigkeit, Ehrlichkeit, Disziplin,
Zielstrebigkeit, Pünktlichkeit.

Shopping

Ich möchte (Karotten/Trauben/Zahnpasta/Joghurt/Brot/
Erbsen) kaufen. Ich hätte gerne (eine Flasche Limonade).
Ich habe (zweihundert Gramm Weichkäse) gekauft. Wo
finde ich (die Lebensmittelabteilung)? (Im ersten
Stock/im Erdgeschoss). Was kostet das?/Was kosten sie?
Kann ich mit Kreditkarte bezahlen? Das ist (zu groß/zu
klein/zu teuer) für mich. Ich habe (diesen Rock/diese
Bluse/dieses Schreibset/diese Gläser) gekauft und
(er/sie/es ist/sie sind) (zu klein/zu groß/die falsche Farbe).
Kann ich (ihn/sie/es/sie) bitte umtauschen?

Describing people

Kannst du (deine Eltern/deinen Lehrer/deine Lehrerin/ deinen Freund/deine Freundin) beschreiben? Sind sie/ist er/sie (fleißig/nett/humorlos/schüchtern/komisch/doof/ praktisch)? Ist das ein guter Freund/eine gute Freundin)?

The environment

Was machst du für die Umwelt? Das ist ein großes Problem. Wir sortieren unseren Müll, so dass er recycelt werden kann. Wir kompostieren unsere organischen Abfälle. Ich gehe so oft wie möglich zu Fuß. Das hilft die Verschmutzung zu vermindern. Die Verlust an Bäumen trägt dazu bei, den Treibhauseffekt zu verschlechtern.

Informal letters

Liebe Heidi!/Lieber Franz! Schreib mir bald (wieder)/bis bald/mit bestem Gruß/viele Grüße Dein Max/Deine Natalie

Formal letters

Sehr geehrte Frau Schilling!/Sehr geehrter Herr Bauchmann! hochachtungsvoll/mit freundlichen Grüßen/mit bestem Dank im Voraus für ihre Hilfe/ihre Bemühungen, Markus Schiffer/Marianne Lenken

Your past

Ich habe (7) Jahre an der (Realschule Bad Marienberg) studiert. Da habe ich (Französisch, Englisch, Mathematik, Deutsch, Physik, Chemie, Erdkunde) gelernt. Letzen Sommer habe ich Zeit im Ausland verbracht. Ich bin durch Europa gefahren! Das hat wirklich Spaß gemacht. Ich habe in verschiedenen Orten als (Kellner/in) gearbeitet. Ich habe ein bisschen Geld dafür verdient. Meine Eltern haben mir finanziell geholfen.

Remember

Always use three tenses: past (ich habe ... gemacht/gekauft/verbracht/gespielt; ich bin nach ... gefahren); **present** (ich interessiere mich für ...; ich habe ...; ich bin ...); **and future** (wir werden nach ... fahren; nächste Woche/nächstes Jahr fahre ich nach ... /mache ich ... /lerne ich ...).

Express your opinion: (das gefällt mir sehr gut/überhaupt nicht; ich mag das nicht; ich finde das sehr schön/nicht gut).

Say why you think that: (weil ... (nicht) sehr (nett/interessant/langweilig/schwierig/komisch, ist).

When you do any writing, go back and check:

- that you have used the right form of the verb – <u>ich</u> wohn<u>e</u>
- that all your nouns begin with a capital letter – das <u>H</u>aus
- that your verb is in the right place (make sure you know all the words/sentence forms that send the verb to the end and remember the verb is always the second idea)
- that any noun, pronoun or adjective describing that noun is in the right case (accusative, dative, etc.) and has the right word for 'the' or 'a' (nouns), the right form (pronouns) and the right ending (adjectives)
- that you have used the right part of **haben** or **sein** when you use the past tense.
- Try to use as much of the language you know as possible. Remember you are supposed to be showing off your skill and impressing the examiners.
- Learn some sentences about each topic by heart, so that you can use them correctly in both written and spoken form.
- Always be certain you do everything you are asked to do – don't miss out any parts. If you don't know, have a guess.